Cooking for Friends

Nanette Newman has made an international reputation in two careers. The star of a score of films and television series, she is the author of over thirty children's books and six previous cookbooks, and is published in many countries. Her *Summer Cookbook* won the Cookbook of the Year Award. She is married to film director and author, Bryan Forbes.

GW00631020

Cooking
for Friends
with
Nanette Newman

Mandarin

**This book
is for Gillian
who constantly
saves my bacon**

A Mandarin Paperback

COOKING FOR FRIENDS

First published in Great Britain 1991
by Mandarin Paperbacks
Michelin House, 81 Fulham Road, London SW3 6RB

Mandarin is an imprint of the Octopus Publishing Group,
a division of Reed International Books Limited

Copyright © Bryan Forbes Limited 1991

A CIP catalogue record for this title
is available from the British Library
ISBN 0 7493 0640 8

Typeset by Falcon Typographic Art Ltd,
Edinburgh & London
Printed and bound in Great Britain
by Cox & Wyman Ltd, Reading, Berks

This book is sold subject to the condition
that it shall not, by way of trade or otherwise,
be lent, resold, hired out, or otherwise circulated
without the publisher's prior consent in any form
of binding or cover other than that in which
it is published and without a similar condition
including this condition being imposed
on the subsequent purchaser.

Contents

Foreword

Do you, like me, sometimes find that there are days when you have friends coming to dinner, for lunch or the weekend or whatever, and you stand in the kitchen, you stare at the fridge and the cupboards and your brain goes blank?

You do? Good. I'm glad I'm not alone. It's on days like these that you reach for a cookbook (hopefully mine) in order to spark off your imagination and give you a bit of enthusiasm to start cooking.

So many things have happened since I first began to cook (as a very young wife whose idea of a successful meal was tinned soup that didn't burn!). Today we are all into health foods and diets; we are reminded of cholesterol and calories at every turn; we read about additives and sprays; should we trust eggs?; what about meat?; and then there's the battle of butter versus spreads. In short, we are bombarded with varying bits of conflicting and ever-changing information. Alongside this, entertaining at home has also changed: no longer do we feel compelled to serve that inevitably boring three-course meal every time we have a dinner party – we do our own thing, we create our own style and cook the way which suits us, our family and friends. We don't want to be tied to the kitchen, red-faced, cross and exhausted, but we do want to serve delicious food.

Well, this book is for people like that – people like me. I have combined my Christmas and Summer cookbooks, added lots of extra things, ideas and recipes and, I think – I hope – there is a bit of something for everyone.

This book is not a book of specialised recipes, it is a pot-pourri of things I've enjoyed, recipes I've collected, concocted or been given, and which have given pleasure to the people I've cooked them for. They have helped me survive those dog days when the phone is ringing, the children are shouting, the plumber can't come, the car won't start and the kitten has chewed the shopping list, and people need to be fed.

I hope you enjoy it.

Nanette Newman

Useful Facts and Figures

Metrication Throughout this book I have given quantities in both metric and imperial measures. Since exact conversion from imperial to metric does not usually give practical working quantities, the metric measures have been rounded to the nearest unit of 25 grams. The table below gives the recommended equivalents. However, remember that when making any of the recipes in this book, follow *only* one set of measures as they are not interchangeable.

Ounce	Recommended conversion to nearest unit of 25 grams
1	25
2	50
3	75
4	100
5	150
6	175
7	200
8	225
9	250
10	275
11	300
12	350
13	375
14	400
15	425
16 (1 lb)	450

Liquid Measures The millilitre has been used in this book and the following table gives a few examples:

Imperial	Recommended millilitre conversion	American cup measure conversion
¼ pint	150 ml	⅔ cup
½ pint	300 ml	1 ¼ cups
¾ pint	450 ml	scant 2 cups
1 pint	600 ml	2 ½ cups

Spoon Measures Spoon measures are level unless otherwise stated.

Egg Sizes All eggs used refer to size 3 unless otherwise stated. When large eggs are used this refers to sizes 1 or 2.

Quantities I have suggested how many people each recipe will serve, but naturally, it depends upon your own assessment of your friends' appetites.

Seasonings Throughout the book I have mainly used fresh herbs but should you use dried, then just remember to halve the quantities.

We are all health-conscious today and many of us wish to cut down on salt, therefore I have not given salt and pepper quantities — this is best left to your own taste and conscience.

Stocks There is no doubt that home-made stock is by far the best, but don't go into intensive care if you have to use a stock cube. We all do it occasionally.

Fats Should you prefer to substitute margarine for butter in the recipes they will still work.

Oven Temperatures Here are the recommended equivalents:

	C	F	gas mark
Very cool	110	225	1/4
	120	250	1/2
Cool	140	275	1
	150	300	2
Moderate	160	325	3
	180	350	4
Moderately hot	190	375	5
	200	400	6
Hot	220	425	7
	230	450	8
Very hot	240	475	9

The oven should always be heated to the required temperature before baking.

Good Beginnings

The following recipes are starters – the first course for the traditional three-course dinner. However, should you – like me – frequently break with tradition and serve just a main course, then you might care to think of the following starters as light lunches or suppers instead.

So, although the choice of how you use them is yours – we'll begin at the beginning.

Split Pea and Apple Soup
Serves 6 to 8

450 g / 1 lb split peas
1 ham bone
2 large onions, cut in chunks
1 cooking apple, peeled, cored and chopped
2.4 litres / 4 pints chicken stock
Salt and pepper

Serve with chunks of hot granary bread on a cold day.

Soak the split peas for 1 hour, then drain and rinse them and remove any odd-looking specimens. Put the peas in a large saucepan with all the other ingredients. Bring to the boil, reduce the heat and simmer, covered, for about 1 hour until tender. Skim the soup occasionally.

When the peas are soft, remove the ham bone and add seasoning to taste. Blend the soup in batches in a liquidiser or food processor and reheat before serving.

Curried Parsnip Soup
Serves 6

40 g / 1½ oz butter
2 onions, chopped
2 teaspoons peeled and chopped fresh root ginger
¼ teaspoon ground coriander
generous pinch each of cayenne pepper, turmeric, ground cumin and nutmeg
450 g / 1 lb parsnips (when peeled and chopped)
1 potato, peeled and chopped
1¾ pints chicken stock
salt
curry powder (optional)
150 ml / ¼ pint soured cream (optional)

Melt the butter in a large saucepan. Add the chopped onions and cook gently until very soft but not browned. Stir in the ginger and spices, then fry for 1 minute, stirring constantly. Stir in the parsnips and potatoes and continue to stir-fry for a minute. Pour in the stock, give the soup a stir, then bring to the boil. Cover the pan and simmer gently for about 45 minutes until the vegetables are soft.

Blend the cooked soup until smooth in batches in a liquidiser, and return it to the pan. Reheat the soup thoroughly and taste for seasoning, adding a little salt or curry powder as necessary, then stir in the cream, if used. Serve very hot. This soup freezes well.

Tomato and Mozzarella Salad
Serves 4

This is so simple, but delicious if the tomatoes are at their best.

6 large very ripe tomatoes, thinly sliced
some walnut oil or best-quality olive oil
mozzarella cheese, thinly sliced
a handful of basil leaves, chopped
Italian bread to serve

Arrange the tomatoes on a dish, drizzle with oil, add salt and pepper, top with mozzarella and sprinkle with basil leaves. Serve with Italian bread.

Iced Apricot Soup
Serves 6

1.5 kg / 3 lb apricots
450 ml / ¾ pint sweet white wine
1 cinnamon stick
150 ml / ¼ pint single cream
about 3–4 tablespoons natural yogurt

This is equally good with peaches instead of apricots

Halve the apricots and remove their stones. Put them in a pan with the wine and cinnamon stick. Bring to the boil and simmer gently until the fruit is very soft. Purée in a liquidiser or food processor, then sieve the soup and leave to cool completely.

Stir in the cream and chill for about an hour. Stir in the yogurt just before serving, or swirl it on top. *Note*: To go with this soup make some miniature muffins. Follow the recipe for Breakfast Muffins on page 164 but cook the mixture in very small bun tins and shorten the time so that the muffins do not overcook.

Melon Soup
Serves 4 to 6

I love cold summer soups — the simplest are made by pulverising fruit (sieved if the fruit has pips) and stirring in natural yogurt. Serve thoroughly chilled

1 very ripe melon
a good pinch of cinnamon
2 cups freshly squeezed orange juice
2 tablespoons lemon juice
sprigs of mint, finely chopped

Pulverise the melon, add to the orange juice and stir in the cinnamon and lemon juice. Add finely chopped mint. Chill thoroughly before serving.

Creamed Carrot Soup
Serves 6 to 8

Try substituting root artichokes for the carrots — and a grating of fresh nutmeg.

50 g/2 oz butter
2 onions, finely chopped
2 sticks celery, finely chopped
1 kg/2 lb carrots, thinly sliced
2 potatoes, thinly sliced
600 ml/1 pint chicken stock
1 teaspoon sugar
salt and pepper
300 ml/½ pint milk
150 ml/¼ pint single cream (optional)
GARNISH
chopped fresh mint
grated carrot

Melt the butter in a saucepan, add the chopped onions and celery and sauté until the vegetables are soft but not brown. Add the sliced carrots and potatoes and quickly toss these in the butter with the other vegetables. Pour in the chicken stock then stir in the sugar and seasoning to taste. Bring the soup to the boil, turn down the heat and simmer gently for about 15 minutes until the carrots are soft.

Pour batches of the soup into a liquidiser or food processor and purée the ingredients with the milk until smooth. Allow the soup to cool, then chill it thoroughly. Stir in the milk and cream (if used) and re-chill the soup. Serve, garnished with chopped mint and grated carrot.

Alternatively, to serve hot, reheat the soup gently, making sure that it does not boil (or the cream will curdle) and serve topped with a little extra cream.

Quick Broccoli Soup
Serves 6

2 (227 g/8 oz) packets frozen broccoli
1.15 litres/2 pints chicken stock
1 onion, chopped
2 sticks celery, chopped
salt and pepper
up to 150 ml/¼ pint milk

Watercress can be used in this recipe instead of the broccoli. Use 2 bunches watercress, trimmed, and prepare as above. Chill the purée before stirring in some cream.

Put the broccoli in a saucepan with the stock, chopped onion and celery; bring to the boil, then lower the heat, cover and simmer for 10 minutes.

Blend the soup in batches, in a liquidiser or food processor, until smooth. Return the soup to the saucepan. Season to taste, add enough milk to make the consistency you like and mix thoroughly. Reheat slowly without allowing the soup to boil, then serve with croûtons (cubes of bread, fried in a mixture of butter and oil until crisp and golden).

Hasty Vegetable Soup
Serves 4 to 6

50 g/2 oz butter
2 onions, chopped
2 courgettes, chopped
2 sticks celery, chopped
750 ml/1¼ pints chicken stock
1 (225 g/8 oz) packet frozen peas
1 tablespoon chopped fresh parsley
a little single cream to serve (optional)

Melt the butter in a saucepan, add the chopped onions, courgettes and celery and cook over a moderate heat for about 8 minutes until soft. Add the chicken stock and peas, then bring to the boil and simmer for 10 minutes. Leave to cool.

This soup can be served hot or cold, garnished with the chopped parsley. To serve it cold, add some cream (if used) and chill the soup. Alternatively, reheat the soup, then add the cream just before serving, but do not allow the soup to boil.

Cold Tomato Soup with Basil
Serves 4

1 kg/2 lb ripe tomatoes
½ teaspoon sugar
1 tablespoon chopped basil
150 ml/¼ pint crème fraîche
1 teaspoon Tabasco sauce
salt and pepper

Put the tomatoes into a bowl, pour on boiling water and leave for a minute. Drain, peel and remove the seeds. Put the tomatoes in a liquidiser or food processor and add all the other ingredients. Purée until smooth, then chill thoroughly before serving.

Alternatively, put the tomato purée in the freezer, freeze until slushy, then whisk thoroughly and re-freeze until firm. Serve scooped into dishes.

Sunshine Soup
Serves 4 to 6

450 g/1 lb carrots, chopped
1 large onion, chopped
25 g/1 oz butter
grated rind and juice of 2 oranges
600 ml/1 pint chicken stock
salt and pepper
glass of dry sherry
little cream or yogurt to taste

Cook the carrots and onions in the butter for about 8 to 10 minutes, stirring frequently so that the onion softens. Add the orange rind and juice, then pour in the stock and bring to the boil. Cover and simmer for 30 minutes.

Blend the soup in a liquidiser and sprinkle in seasoning to taste with the sherry. Chill the soup thoroughly before stirring in the cream and serving.

Consommé with Soured Cream and Caviar
Serves 5 to 6

2 (411 g/14½ oz) cans Crosse and Blackwell beef consommé
150 ml/¼ pint soured cream
1 (99 g/3½ oz) jar caviar or lumpfish roe
lemon slices, to garnish

Pour the consommé into five or six wide-necked glasses and place them in the refrigerator until set – 3 to 4 hours. Alternatively, chill the soup in one large bowl until set, then spoon it into the glasses.

Top each portion with a little soured cream and a spoonful of caviar or lumpfish roe. Garnish with lemon slices and serve ice-cold. Hand hot toast separately, or serve with herbed bread.

Chop two or three of your favourite herbs – mix about a handful of each with softened butter.

Slice a French loaf diagonally, leaving the slices attached at the base, then butter them and press the loaf back together. Top with sprigs of fresh herbs and pack the loaf in cooking foil, then bake in a mod. hot oven (190C, 375F, gas 5) for 15 to 20 minutes.

Consommé with Cream Cheese
Serves 6

1 tablespoon sherry
7 g/¼ oz gelatine
2 (411 g/14½ oz) cans Crosse and Blackwell beef consommé
275 g/10 oz Philadelphia cream cheese

Warm the sherry and dissolve the gelatine into it. Blend the mixture with the consommé in a liquidiser or food processor. Reserve a quarter of the consommé for the topping, then blend the remaining soup with the cheese. Pour into six individual ramekins and chill until set. Dissolve the reserved consommé but do not allow it to become too hot, then pour a thin layer over the soup in each ramekin. Return to the refrigerator until the consommé is set. Serve with hot toast.

Smoked Salmon and Watercress Mousse
Serves 4 to 6

Fresh or frozen smoked salmon trimmings can be bought cheaply from some fishmongers or delicatessens

350 g/12 oz smoked salmon pieces
350 g/12 oz cottage cheese
150 ml/¼ pint soured cream
2 tablespoons lemon juice
salt and pepper
cayenne pepper
4 bunches watercress
2 tablespoons mayonnaise
TO DECORATE
curls of smoked salmon
sprigs of watercress
lemon slices

Roughly chop the smoked salmon, then put the pieces into a liquidiser or food processor with 100 g/4 oz of the cottage cheese, the soured cream and lemon juice (you may need to do this in several batches). Process until smooth and season to taste with salt and cayenne. Tip the purée into a bowl.

Pick all the leaves off the watercress and discard the stalks. Plunge the leaves into boiling water for 10 seconds. Drain, rinse with cold water, then drain thoroughly, squeezing out the excess liquid. Blend the watercress with the remaining cottage cheese and mayonnaise in a liquidiser or food processor until smooth. Season with salt and pepper.

Pour a third of the salmon mixture into a glass serving bowl. Cover with half the watercress mixture. Repeat, then top with a layer of the salmon mixture. Cover and chill until ready to serve.

If you wish, the mousse can be decorated with curls of smoked salmon, sprigs of watercress and lemon slices. Serve with hot wholewheat rolls or toast.

Shrimp and Sherry Starter
Serves 6

1 onion, finely chopped
75 g/3 oz butter
6 canned tomatoes, drained and chopped
6 mushrooms, chopped
6 (100 g/4 oz) cartons potted shrimps
2 tablespoons double cream
dash of sherry
6 slices white bread, with crusts removed
1 tablespoon oil
chopped parsley

Sauté the finely chopped onion in half the butter for about 5 minutes until soft. Add the tomatoes and mushrooms and stir for a minute over a moderate heat. Next stir in the potted shrimps, cream and a good dash of sherry and warm through gently.

Fry the bread slices in the remaining butter and the oil, turning them once, until golden brown on both sides. Top the bread with the shrimp mixture and serve immediately, sprinkled with chopped parsley.

Easy Fish Terrine
Serves 6

225 g/8 oz cooked salmon, kippers, smoked haddock, fresh or smoked trout, or smoked mackerel
3 canned anchovy fillets, drained
100 g/4 oz unsalted butter, softened
a little lemon juice
cayenne pepper
75 g/3 oz butter, melted for topping

Blend all the ingredients except the melted butter together in a food processor or mash them with a fork and beat until smooth. Taste for seasoning and *A few strips of chervil or dill to decorate* adjust it if necessary by adding more lemon juice or cayenne. Press the pâté into ramekins or one large dish and pour the melted butter over to form a seal. Chill until firm. Serve with hot toast.

Egg and Asparagus
Serves 6

about 30 asparagus tips, cooked and drained
6 hard-boiled eggs
6 tablespoons double cream
pepper
100 g/4 oz grated cheese
50 g/2 oz chopped salted peanuts

You can use tinned asparagus if the fresh isn't in season.

Place four or five asparagus tips in each of six individual ovenproof dishes. Quarter the eggs lengthways and arrange the pieces in neat rows on top of the asparagus, white side up. Pour a tablespoonful of cream over each of the eggs. Season, then sprinkle with grated cheese and chopped peanuts.

Place the dishes in a moderately hot oven (190C, 375F, gas 5) for 5 to 10 minutes, or until the top is lightly browned (care must be taken not to overcook this dish). Serve immediately.

Stuffed Pasta Shells
Serves 4

225 g/8 oz large pasta shells
1 large tub cottage cheese
2 eggs
1 onion, finely chopped
½ green pepper, deseeded and finely chopped
1 (198 g/7 oz) can tuna, drained
25 g/1 oz butter
25 g/1 oz fresh breadcrumbs

Bring a large saucepan of salted water to the boil, add the pasta shells and simmer gently until the pasta is just tender. Rinse in cold water and drain thoroughly.

Mix all the remaining ingredients together apart from the butter and breadcrumbs. Carefully fill the shells with the cottage cheese mixture and place them in a greased baking dish. Dot with butter and sprinkle with breadcrumbs. Cover with cooking foil and bake in a moderate oven (180c, 350f, gas 4) for 20 minutes.

At the end of the cooking time remove the foil covering and brown the stuffed pasta under the grill. Serve immediately.

Special Macaroni Cheese
Serves 6

225 g/8 oz macaroni
65 g/2½ oz butter
40 g/1½ oz flour
450 ml/¾ pint milk
100 g/4 oz lean cooked ham, cut into strips
4 large tomatoes, peeled and chopped
175 g/6 oz cheese, grated
salt and pepper
2 tablespoons fresh breadcrumbs

Cook the macaroni in plenty of simmering, salted water for 10 to 12 minutes or until just tender, then drain.

Meanwhile melt 40 g/1½ oz of the butter, add the flour and stir till blended, then add the milk and cook over a low heat, whisking continuously, until the sauce thickens. Let the sauce simmer for a few minutes.

Stir the macaroni, ham, tomatoes and 100 g/4 oz of the cheese into the sauce. Season well. Transfer to buttered individual ovenproof dishes. Mix the remaining cheese with the breadcrumbs and sprinkle over the top of the macaroni. Dot the surface with the remaining butter and bake in a moderately hot oven (200c, 400f, gas 6) for 20 minutes or until the cheese topping is crisp and golden. Serve immediately.

If you have this as a starter, you really only need a salad as a main course. When serving place a folded napkin on a dinner plate before placing the oven proof dish on top.

Pâté in Brioche

FOR EACH SERVING ALLOW:
1 brioche
15 g / ½ oz softened butter
about 50 g / 2 oz pâté
shredded lettuce or watercress to serve

Cut the cap off the brioche and scoop out the soft crumb from the centre. Spread the inside with the softened butter and heat in a moderate oven (180C, 350F, gas 4) for about 10 minutes until crisp. Cool.

Fill with your favourite pâté and replace the cap. Serve on a bed of shredded lettuce or watercress.

Chicken Pâté

Serves 6

450 g / 1 lb breast of chicken, skinned and roughly chopped
2 egg whites
4 tablespoons double cream
450 g / 1 lb broccoli, cooked and puréed
salt and pepper
salad ingredients to garnish;
for example cucumber, radishes and tomatoes

Purée chicken in a liquidiser or food processor. Add the egg whites and half the cream and blend until smooth. Stir the broccoli purée into the mixture, adding salt and pepper to taste. Fold in rest of the cream.

Pour the pâté into a suitable ovenproof serving dish. Cover the dish and stand it in a large roasting tin. Pour in hot water to come halfway up the side of the dish. Cover with cooking foil and cook in a moderate oven (160C, 325F, gas 3) for 1½ hours. Cool and chill overnight.

Turn out on to a platter and serve surrounded by different types of lettuce.

Bloody Mary Starter
Serves 4

juice of 2 lemons
250 ml/8 fl oz tomato juice
3 tablespoons vodka
pinch of salt
a few drops of Worcestershire sauce (or to taste)
freshly ground black pepper
1 egg white
4 ice cubes, crushed
lemon slices to decorate

Place all the ingredients in a liquidiser or food processor and blend until frothy. Pour into a suitable container and put in the freezer. After 30 minutes give the mixture a good stir, then cover and return the container to the freezer and leave until the mixture is solid.

To serve, transfer the container to the refrigerator for 30 minutes. Spoon into chilled wine glasses and decorate with lemon slices.

Avocado Starter
Serves 6

3 ripe avocado pears
3 sticks celery
3 spring onions (optional)
1 tart dessert apple
3 tablespoons mayonnaise
salt and pepper

Cut the avocados in half and remove the stones. Scoop out the flesh, leaving the shell intact. Chop the flesh. Cut the celery into matchsticks, and put these into ice cold water for a few minutes to crisp up. Slice the spring onions (if used) and add them to the chopped avocado. Dice the apple, then stir it into the avocado mixture with the drained celery and the mayonnaise. Season to taste. Spoon the mixture into the avocado shells and serve immediately.

Obviously home-made mayonnaise is the nicest!

Stuffed Whole Avocados
Serves 6

6 ripe avocado pears
2 tablespoons lemon juice
175 g/6 oz Philadelphia cream cheese
2 tablespoons chopped canned pimiento
1 tablespoon finely chopped chives
salt and pepper
Tabasco sauce

Use a very sharp knife to slice the avocados because it's important the slices don't look messy.

Cut the avocados in half across the middle (not lengthways). Twist the halves to separate them, then brush the cut surfaces with lemon juice to prevent discoloration. Carefully remove the avocado stones and brush the hollows with lemon juice.

Mix the Philadelphia cheese with the pimiento and chives. Season to taste with salt, pepper and Tabasco, then stuff the avocados with this mixture by pressing the cheese into the holes left by the stones. Put the avocado halves back together and wrap each avocado in cling film. Chill until ready to eat.

Peel the avocados, then thinly slice them into rings. Arrange the slices on individual plates, then serve with Vinaigrette Dressing (page 78) and Quick Walnut Bread (page 163).

Crab and Grapefruit
Serves 8

1 (215 g/7½ oz) packet frozen puff pastry, defrosted
1 egg, beaten
225g/8 oz cream cheese
4 tablespoons soured cream
¼ teaspoon paprika
4 pink grapefruit
225g/8 oz crab meat
salt and pepper
SAUCE
2 ripe avocado pears
150 ml/¼ pint soured cream
bunch of chives, chopped
a few drops of lemon juice

GARNISH

sprigs of lemon balm

some Iceberg lettuce, shredded

Roll out the pastry very thinly into an oblong shape measuring about 15 × 50 cm/6 × 20 in, then cut it into four pieces. Prick the pastry all over with a fork, lay the pieces on baking trays and glaze them with some of the beaten egg. Bake in a hot oven (230c, 450f, gas 8) for 10 to 12 minutes. Transfer to wire racks to cool.

Beat the cream cheese with the soured cream and paprika. Grate the rind from one of the grapefruit and add to the cream cheese mixture. Cut all the peel and pith off the fruit, then cut between the membranes and remove the segments (if you do this over a bowl you will catch all the juice). Flake the crab meat and mix it with the fruit segments, adding seasoning.

To make the sauce, halve, peel and stone the avocados, then mash them until smooth and add the soured cream, chives, and lemon juice. Blend well and chill quickly in the freezer.

Spread the pastry with the cream cheese mixture, then top with the crab meat and grapefruit, and lemon balm. Arrange on a serving dish and surround with the shredded lettuce. Eat topped with the avocado sauce. Follow this with a sorbet and you have a delicious lunch.

Savoury Jelly
Serves 6 to 8

600 ml/1 pint white grape juice

25 g/1 oz gelatine

a few sprigs of mint

1½ cucumbers

2 tablespoons white wine vinegar

225 g/8 oz seedless white grapes

salt and pepper

Use about 6 tablespoons of the grape juice to dissolve the gelatine over a low heat.

Roughly chop the mint and add it to the remaining grape juice and the dissolved gelatine. Peel and coarsely grate the cucumbers, squeeze out all the excess liquid, add the vinegar and stir then add to the grape juice. Halve or quarter the grapes if they are large, add to the mixture. Add seasoning to taste and pour into a 1.4 litre/2½ pint mould. Chill until set.

Stuffed Apples
Serves 4

Useful for a light lunch or as an unusual starter.

2 large smoked mackerel fillets, flaked
2 hard-boiled eggs, chopped
bunch of parsley, chopped
bunch of chives, chopped
salt and pepper
about 3 tablespoons soured cream
1 tablespoon mayonnaise
1 generous tablespoon creamed horseradish
4 large crisp dessert apples
a little lemon juice

Cut inside the apples carefully, they are a bit tricky to do — especially if they are small so try and use large ones.

Make sure there are no bones or pieces of skin in the flaked mackerel, then mix it with the eggs, herbs and seasoning to taste. Add the soured cream, mayonnaise and horseradish.

Cut the tops off the apples and keep these for lids. Scoop out the apples with a small sharp knife to leave hollow shells and sprinkle the insides with a little lemon juice to prevent them from turning brown. Cut the apple flesh into cubes discarding the cores, then add the fruit to the mackerel mixture. Stir well, use to fill the apples, then replace the lids. Serve soon after the apples are filled.

Note: The mackerel and egg mixture can be prepared the evening before, if you like, ready to have the apple mixed in at the last minute.

Baked Aubergine Slices
Serves 4

2 large aubergines
salt and pepper
175 g/6 oz fresh wholemeal breadcrumbs
75 g/3 oz Emmental or Cheddar cheese, grated
6–8 tablespoons mayonnaise

Trim the ends off the aubergines, then slice them lengthways. (If you have time salt the slices and put in a sieve to drain. Then rinse and pat dry.)

Mix the breadcrumbs with the cheese and put the mixture in a thick layer on a plate. Spread both sides of the aubergine slices with mayonnaise, then press into the cheese and breadcrumb mixture so that both sides are thickly coated. Place on a greased baking tray. Bake in a moderately hot oven (200C, 400F, gas 6) for 25 to 30 minutes, or until brown and crisp. Sprinkle with chopped parsley. Serve hot as a first course, or for lunch with a salad.

Never we bought breadcrumbs — they always taste horrid ~ I think!

Mackerel Pots
Serves 4

50 g/2 oz butter
handful of oatflakes
grated rind of 1 lemon
4 smoked mackerel fillets
4 tablespoons mayonnaise
juice of 1 lemon
4 hard-boiled eggs, chopped
salt and pepper
lemon balm sprigs, to garnish

Melt the butter in a pan, then add the oatflakes and cook over a low heat, stirring frequently until lightly browned. Stir in the lemon rind and remove the pan from the heat.

Skin and flake the mackerel, then add it to the oatflakes with the mayonnaise and lemon juice. Stir in the eggs and plenty of seasoning, then put the mixture into individual ovenproof pots or dishes and bake in a moderately hot oven (200C, 400F, gas 6) for 8 to 10 minutes. Garnish with lemon balm sprigs and serve with hot wholemeal toast.

Savoury Stuffed Pears

WALNUT AND ROQUEFORT

Serves 4

4 large ripe pears
100 g/4 oz Roquefort cheese, mashed
50 g/2 oz chopped walnuts
1 tablespoon mayonnaise
1 tablespoon brandy
25 g/1 oz walnuts, chopped
GARNISH
walnut halves
sprigs of watercress

Core the whole pears from the underneath, leaving their stalks in place. Mix the cheese with the chopped walnuts, mayonnaise and brandy, to make a creamy paste. Press this stuffing into the cavities from the cores, then serve one stuffed pear per person, garnished with walnut halves and watercress.

If preparing in advance, brush the pears with lemon juice to stop them from turning brown. Serve with Ginger Thins (page 213).

Peculiar Fruit Salad

Select as many different fruits as possible – the more the better. Prepare the fruit according to its type, then arrange it attractively on a large dish. In a screw-topped jar, mix 3 tablespoons lemon juice, 2 tablespoons each of sunflower oil and olive oil, 1 tablespoon cider vinegar, 1 dessertspoon clear honey, 1 dessertspoon poppy seeds and seasoning to taste. Shake well and pour this dressing over the fruit. Chill for 30 minutes before serving.

Served with cottage cheese this makes a delicious lunch.

PORT AND STILTON

Serves 8

| 4 large ripe pears, peeled and halved |
| 100 g/4 oz ripe Stilton cheese |
| 2 tablespoons port |
| 2 tablespoons cream cheese |
| watercress, to garnish |

Core the pears. Mash the Stilton with the port and cream cheese. Spoon this filling into the pears and garnish with watercress.

In all the recipes calling for cream cheese, I always use the "light" lower-calorie one.

Pineapple, Avocado and Yogurt Salad
Serves 4

| 1 ripe pineapple |
| 1 ripe avocado pear, peeled, stoned and thinly sliced |
| a small bunch of grapes, halved and stoned |
| 50 g/2 oz pistachio nuts, shelled and chopped |
| 300 ml/½ pint natural yogurt |
| 2 teaspoons freshly chopped mint |
| 1 small lettuce, shredded |

Cut the pineapple in half lengthways. Cut out the flesh, remove the core and chop the fruit into chunks. Mix the fruit with the avocado, grapes, most of the pistachios, the yogurt and mint. Mix well and chill. Serve on lettuce, garnished with the reserved nuts.

Note: When very small pineapples are in the shops I serve one per person. Slice the top off the pineapple, then scoop out and chop the flesh, discarding the core. Mix the fruit with the other ingredients as above, then spoon the salad back into the pineapple shells and replace the lids. Decorate the top by placing fresh flowers in amongst the leaves.

Pepper and Anchovy Salad
Serves 6

1 (50 g/1¾ oz) can anchovy fillets
3 tablespoons olive oil
knob of butter
2 tablespoons double cream
6 red or green peppers

Pound the anchovies in a pestle and mortar or purée them until smooth. Heat 2 tablespoons of the oil and the butter in a small frying pan, add the anchovies and cook for a few minutes. Tip into a liquidiser, add the cream and blend until smooth.

You can roast the peppers and skin them if you prefer.

Cut the tops off the peppers and remove all the seeds. Drop the peppers into a large pan of boiling water, adding the remaining oil, and simmer for 5 minutes.

Drain the peppers and arrange them on a serving dish, whole, halved or sliced. Serve the fairly small amount of the rich anchovy sauce in a small bowl to accompany the peppers, and offer hot French bread as an accompaniment.

Spiced Aubergine with Tomato
Serves 6

1 aubergine
3 tablespoons lemon juice
175 g/6 oz flour
1 egg
250 ml/8 fl oz milk
oil for frying
1 (397 g/14 oz) can chopped tomatoes
2 cloves garlic, crushed
salt and pepper
pinch of nutmeg
¼ teaspoon dried mixed herbs
2 teaspoons cider vinegar
1 teaspoon sugar
175 g/6 oz mozzarella cheese, grated

Slice the aubergine thinly and sprinkle the slices with lemon juice. Sift 100 g/4 oz of the flour into a bowl, make a well in the middle and add the egg. Gradually pour in the milk and beat thoroughly to make a smooth batter. Toss the aubergine slices in the rest of the flour, then dip them in the batter and shallow fry them for 2 minutes on each side or until golden. Remove the aubergine slices from the frying pan and drain them on absorbent kitchen paper.

Mix the tomatoes, garlic, seasoning, nutmeg, herbs, cider vinegar and sugar. Place half the aubergine slices into six individual ovenproof dishes or one large dish. Cover with a layer of the tomato mixture and mozzarella cheese, then top with a second layer of aubergines, the remaining tomatoes and finally top with the last of the cheese.

Place in a moderate oven (160c, 325f, gas 3) for 30 minutes or until the cheese is melted and lightly browned.

Serve with hot French bread.

Spinach Tarts
Serves 8

250 g/9 oz flour
100 g/4 oz unsalted butter
2 egg yolks
generous pinch of salt
3–4 tablespoons cold water
100 g/4 oz rindless streaky bacon, chopped
freshly ground black pepper
grated nutmeg
350 g/12 oz frozen chopped spinach, defrosted and thoroughly drained
225 g/8 oz cottage cheese
3 eggs, beaten
2 tablespoons grated Parmesan or Gruyère cheese

You can omit the bacon from this recipe if you wish.

Sift the flour into a large bowl, then rub in the butter until the mixture resembles fine breadcrumbs. Mix the egg yolks with the salt and 3 tablespoons water. Stir into the flour, using a knife, to make a soft and smooth – but not sticky – dough; add the extra water if the mixture is too dry. Wrap the dough in greaseproof paper and chill until firm.

Roll out the pastry on a floured surface and use to line 8 (7.5 cm/3½ in) tartlet shells. Prick the pastry with a fork and line with greaseproof paper. Sprinkle in some dried peas or beans and bake the pastry case in a hot oven (220c, 425f, gas 7) for 10 to 12 minutes. Take out of the oven, remove the paper and beans and reduce the temperature to moderately hot (190c, 375f, gas 5).

Dry-fry the bacon over a high heat until crisp, stirring constantly, then remove from the pan and season with black pepper and a little nutmeg to taste. Mix with the spinach, add the cottage cheese and eggs and stir to mix thoroughly. Spoon into the pastry cases, sprinkle with grated cheese and bake in the heated oven for 15 minutes or until set.

Prawns with Lime Mayonnaise

This is a very easy way of preparing brunch, lunch or a light supper. Flavour some home-made mayonnaise with the juice and zest of a lime, salt and pepper, chopped parsley and chives. (If you don't make your own mayonnaise, then use the best you can buy.) Pile some halved limes in the middle of a big, flattish dish. Arrange some lettuce hearts and spring onions around them, then put whole cooked Mediterranean prawns all round the edge of the dish. Serve the chilled mayonnaise separately.

Seafood Pâté
Serves 6 to 8

675 g/1½ lb fresh haddock fillet
50 g/2 oz fresh white breadcrumbs
150 ml/¼ pint double cream
grated rind of 2 limes or small lemons
some chopped fennel
2 eggs, separated
salt and pepper
450 g/1 lb peeled cooked prawns

Skin the fish fillet and remove any bones, then mince or whizz it up in a food processor until smooth. Put the fish in a bowl and stir in the breadcrumbs, cream, lime or lemon rind and fennel. Add the egg yolks and mix well, adding plenty of seasoning. Whisk the whites until they stand in stiff peaks, then fold them in carefully.

Chop the prawns and mix them with seasoning. Grease a 1 kg/2 lb loaf tin and line the base with greaseproof paper; grease this thoroughly. Layer the fish and prawn mixtures in the tin, starting and ending with the fish. Stand the pâté in a roasting tin half filled with boiling water. Bake in a moderate oven (180c, 350f, gas 4) for 1 hour. Leave to cool, then chill thoroughly before turning out. Serve with lime mayonnaise (see page 32).

Serve with toasted granary bread.

Salmon Parcels
Serves 4

2 ripe avocado pears
225 g/8 oz Philadelphia cream cheese
dash of Worcestershire sauce
salt and pepper
juice of 1 lemon
2–3 tablespoons soured cream
225 g/8 oz smoked salmon slices
GARNISH
2 small lemons, halved
sprigs of fennel

Halve the pears and remove the stones. Put the flesh in the food processor with the Philadelphia cheese, Worcestershire sauce, seasoning and lemon juice. Add the soured cream and whizz the ingredients together until smooth.

Use the smoked salmon to line four small ramekins leaving the ends of the slices overhanging the edges of the dishes. Press the salmon into the dishes to make sure there are no gaps. Sprinkle with lemon juice and freshly ground black pepper, then divide the avocado mixture between the dishes and fold the ends of the salmon over the top. The mixture should be completely encased. Press lightly, cover with cling film and put in the refrigerator for a couple of hours.

Turn out on to a large plate, one per person. Put a
lemon half on the side and garnish with small sprigs
of fennel. Serve with wholemeal or granary toast.

Cheating Jellied Bortsch
Serves 4 to 6

1 small red onion, finely chopped
350 g/12 oz raw beetroot, finely grated
grated rind and juice of 1 lemon
salt and pepper
2 (411 g/14½ oz) cans consommé
TO SERVE
150 ml/¼ pint soured cream
chopped chives or tarragon

I like to serve this with chunks of black bread

Simply stir all the ingredients together and chill until
set. Fork the jellied mixture, then spoon it into
individual bowls or wine glasses to serve.

Spoon soured cream on top of each serving and top
with chopped chives or tarragon.

Smoked Trout with Guava Dressing
Serves 4

4 smoked trout
4 lettuce hearts
4 limes
DRESSING
3 guavas
150 ml/¼ pint mayonnaise
a few spring onions, chopped
1 tablespoon natural yogurt
salt and pepper

Arrange the smoked trout on individual plates, with
lettuce hearts and a couple of lime halves on each.

Peel the guavas and halve them, then remove the
seeds and stalks. Finely chop the fruit and mix it with
the mayonnaise, onions, yogurt and a little seasoning.
Serve this dressing lightly chilled.

Melon and Mango with Lime

For a light starter, serve wedges of melon with slices of fresh mango. Sprinkle with lime juice and arrange attractively on a serving plate or on individual plates. Add pieces of fresh lime and chill before serving.

Don't serve melon ice cold – it's nice just chilled.

Mozzarella Biscuits

250 g/9 oz plain flour	Makes
large pinch of salt	about 24
1 heaped teaspoon baking powder	(depending
75 g/3 oz butter	on how
300 ml/½ pint buttermilk (you may need a little more)	big your
1 dessertspoon chopped chervil	spoonfuls are)
100 g/4 oz grated mozzarella cheese	

Put the flour, salt, baking powder and butter into a food processor and blend until they resemble breadcrumbs. Add half the buttermilk and the chervil and whizz together until the mixture reaches a dropping consistency, adding more buttermilk if needed. Add the cheese and whizz for 1 second. Drop tablespoons of the mixture on to a greased baking sheet and bake in a preheated, very hot oven (230c, 450f, gas 8) for 15–20 minutes until golden brown. Serve warm.

These are so good to serve with soup or with drinks.

The Main Event

The way you begin and end a meal is rather like the first and last act of a play. Act 1 has everyone seated waiting in anticipation, while the last course is the final curtain, leaving the audience – your guests – feeling that the evening has been well spent. What happens in the middle – the Main Event – is the heart of the matter. I have chosen the following recipes, not only because they taste wonderful for lunch or dinner but because they will stand on their own should you decide to abandon the three-course habit.

You don't have to bother with a starter. Just serve them with salad or vegetables, followed by fruit and cheese instead of a pudding, and you'll still receive rave reviews from your friends.

Stuffed Lemon Sole with White Wine and and Parsley Sauce
Serves 4

8 lemon sole fillets
1 (198 g/7 oz) can tuna or salmon, drained
50 g/2 oz Philadelphia cream cheese
salt and pepper
150 ml/¼ pint white wine
50 g/2 oz butter
25 g/1 oz flour
300 ml/½ pint milk
2 egg yolks
2 tablespoons lemon juice
handful of chopped parsley
parsley or watercress, to garnish

If you can obtain really superb fresh fish don't mess around with it — brush it with some melted butter and herbs and simply grill it. Serve with half a lemon. It can't be beaten.

Remove the black skin from the fish fillets. Put the tuna or salmon, Philadelphia cheese, and seasoning in a liquidiser or food processor and blend until smooth. Place a spoonful of this mixture on each fish fillet (on the skinned side) and roll up. Arrange the fish rolls in a greased ovenproof dish and pour in half the white wine, cover with buttered greaseproof paper and bake in a moderate oven (160c, 325f, gas 3) for 10–20 minutes, depending on the size of the fish. Transfer the fish to a warmed serving dish and keep hot.

Meanwhile, make the wine sauce by combining the butter, flour and milk in a saucepan. Heat until the sauce boils, whisking continuously, then add the cooking juices from the fish and the remaining wine; simmer for 2 minutes.

Take the saucepan off the heat and whisk in the egg yolks, and lemon juice then stir the sauce over a low heat, without allowing it to boil, until thickened. Stir in the chopped parsley and seasoning to taste.

Pour the sauce over the sole, garnish with parsley or watercress and serve immediately.

Special-occasion Lobster
Serves 6

*Simple to make but with a luxurious taste. The lobster
can be fresh (or frozen) or – if you wish – it can be
replaced with cooked fresh salmon or cooked smoked
haddock.*

450 g / 1 lb cooked lobster meat

100 g / 4 oz frozen peeled prawns, thawed

2 hard-boiled eggs, chopped

2 tomatoes, peeled, quartered, deseeded and diced

300 ml / ½ pint mayonnaise

20 g / ¾ oz butter

20 g / ¾ oz flour

300 ml / ½ pint milk

15 g / ½ oz gelatine

2 tablespoons water

300 ml / ½ pint double or whipping cream, whipped

salt and pepper

tomato ketchup, anchovy essence and lemon
   juice to taste

GARNISH

cucumber slices

tomato slices

onion rings

whole shrimps

a little aspic jelly (optional)

Flake the lobster meat and put it into a large bowl with
the prawns, eggs, tomatoes and the mayonnaise.

Melt the butter in a saucepan, stir in the flour,
then gradually stir in the milk. Bring to the boil,
stirring constantly, and simmer for 2 minutes. The
sauce should be smooth and thick.

Dissolve the gelatine in the water in a basin over
a saucepan of hot water, then stir it into the sauce.
Leave the mixture to cool, stirring occasionally, but
do not allow it to set. Mix the sauce into the lobster
mixture with the cream. Add salt and pepper, tomato
ketchup, anchovy essence and lemon juice to taste.

Spoon the mousse into a large glass serving bowl and
chill until set. When set, garnish as wished with any of

the suggested ingredients and spoon a little aspic jelly (if used) over the garnish. Chill again until ready to use. Serve with brown bread and butter.

Smoked Chicken with Avocado and Grapes
Serves 6

1 Iceberg lettuce or small Chinese cabbage, shredded *or* 1 bunch watercress, trimmed and shredded
675 g/1½ lb smoked chicken, cut into strips
225 g/8 oz seedless grapes
1 ripe avocado pear, sliced
75 g/3 oz blanched almonds, toasted until golden
75 ml/3 fl oz soured cream
75 ml/3 fl oz mayonnaise
salt and pepper

There are so many different types of lettuce available — try mixing as many as you like.

Arrange the lettuce, Chinese cabbage or watercress on a large serving plate. Mix the chicken, grapes, sliced avocado and almonds in a bowl. Combine the soured cream, mayonnaise and seasoning to taste, then pour this dressing over the chicken. Fold together gently, pile on top of the lettuce and chill until ready to serve.

Chicken and Peach Salad
Serves 6

2 (411 g/14½ oz) cans white peaches, drained (you can also use ordinary peaches)
300 ml/½ pint mayonnaise
675 g/1½ lb cooked chicken
bunch of spring onions, thinly sliced lengthways
¼ teaspoon dried tarragon
2 teaspoons lemon juice
salt and pepper
1 lettuce
sprigs of parsley, to garnish

Purée two peaches from one can in a liquidiser and blend until smooth, then stir this peach purée into the mayonnaise.

Cut the chicken into strips. Slice the remaining peaches, reserve a few slices for garnish and mix the rest with the chicken and spring onions. Fold into the mayonnaise mixture with the tarragon and lemon juice. Season to taste and mix well.

Wash and dry the lettuce. Arrange the leaves on a serving dish and pile the chicken mixture on top, leaving a border of lettuce showing. Arrange the reserved peaches around the chicken mixture. Garnish with sprigs of parsley or tarragon and serve very cold.

Tipsy Chicken
Serves 6

2 tablespoons oil
25 g/1 oz butter
1 (about 1.5 kg/3 lb in weight) chicken
2 onions, thinly sliced
450 g/1 lb cooking apples, peeled, cored and sliced
175 g/6 oz prunes, stoned (use those which do not require pre-soaking)
6 tablespoons calvados
4 teaspoons flour
600 ml/1 pint chicken stock
salt and pepper
2 bay leaves
4 tablespoons soured cream
GARNISH
450 g/1 lb cooking apples
25 g/1 oz caster sugar
40 g/1½ oz butter

This sounds a bit lengthy, but don't be put off — it's actually very simple

Heat the oil and butter together in a heavy-based flameproof casserole and thoroughly brown the chicken on all sides. Remove the chicken, then lower the heat, add the onions and cook slowly for about 10 minutes until soft but not brown. Add the sliced apples, and stir-fry over a moderate heat until both the apples and the onions are golden brown. Replace the chicken and add the prunes and the calvados, then immediately set the calvados alight. When the flames have died, stir the flour into the juices round the edge of the casserole. Pour in the stock, add seasoning and bay leaves and bring to the boil. Cover and cook in a moderate oven (180c, 350f, gas 4) for 50 minutes or until the chicken is cooked through and tender.

Meanwhile, prepare the garnish. Wash the unpeeled apples, then thickly slice them and neatly remove the cores. Dip the slices in sugar and fry them in the butter (use a non-stick frying pan if possible) until caramelised — about 4 minutes on each side. Keep hot.

Remove the cooked chicken from the casserole and divide it into six portions, or serve it whole if you like; keep it warm. Remove the prunes from the sauce and keep them warm too. Blend the sauce in a liquidiser until smooth — the apples and onions will help to thicken it — then pour it back into the casserole and boil until the sauce is of a coating consistency. Add the soured cream, taste and adjust the seasoning.

Arrange the chicken on a serving dish and garnish with the apple rings and prunes. Spoon a little sauce over the top and serve the rest separately.

Grilled Poussins with Honey and Lemon
Serves 4

4 (each about 450 g / 1 lb in weight) poussins
1½ teaspoons sea salt
4 tablespoons lemon juice
4 tablespoons melted butter
4 tablespoons clear honey
A few slivered almonds

Sprinkle with plenty of lemon balm or tarragon for the last few minutes of cooking.

Use poultry scissors to snip on either side of the backbones in the poussins. Cut out the backbones completely, then turn the birds over and flatten them. Cut off the wing tips and wipe the poussins with a damp cloth. Thread the birds on to skewers to keep them open and flat, then rub them all over with salt and sprinkle with lemon juice. Leave to marinate for 15 minutes.

Brush the poussins with the melted butter and cook them under a hot grill for 25 minutes, turning and basting them frequently. Brush with honey and grill for a further 5 minutes, again basting and turning them

all the time. Sprinkle with the almonds and continue
to grill until golden, then serve very hot, garnished
with lemon wedges, with rice as an accompaniment.
Alternatively, serve the poussins cold with a salad.

Game Pie
Serves 6

*A pie is ideal for using up cooked game. This recipe can
be made from any game – pheasant, woodcock, grouse,
wild duck, pigeon or a mixture. Alternatively, use chicken
or turkey.*

ROUGH PUFF PASTRY

275 g/10 oz plain flour
generous pinch of salt
175 g/6 oz butter, chilled and cut into dice
25 g/1 oz lard or white cooking fat, chilled and cut into dice
175 ml/6 fl oz ice-cold water
1 teaspoon lemon juice

FILLING

450 g/1 lb cooked game free from skin and bone
25 g/1 oz butter
1 small onion, chopped
225 g/8 oz button mushrooms, sliced
2 tablespoons chopped parsley
1 tablespoon flour
175 ml/6 fl oz leftover gravy or well-flavoured stock
salt and pepper
2 hard-boiled eggs
4 rindless rashers streaky bacon, halved
1 (90 g/3½ oz) can pâté de foie gras (optional)
1 egg, beaten

If you don't want to bother to make pastry, buy frozen.

To make the pastry, sift the flour into a bowl with
the salt. Add the fats and, stirring quickly, use a
palette knife to coat the pieces of fat in flour. Mix
the water and lemon juice and stir this liquid into
the flour mixture to make a soft, not sticky, dough
with visible lumps of fat. Turn the dough out on to a

floured surface and shape it into a rectangle. Roll out into a rectangle measuring about 33 × 11 cm/13 × 4½ in, fold the lower third over the middle, then fold the top third down over the first fold. Press the edges together lightly and turn the pastry so that the folded edge is on your left. Re-roll the pastry into a rectangle which is slightly larger than the original one and repeat the folding process. Turn the pastry again and repeat this rolling and folding process four times. Wrap and chill the pastry while you prepare the filling.

Cut the game into bite-sized pieces. Melt the butter in a heavy-based saucepan and cook the onion over a gentle heat with the lid on the saucepan. Stir occasionally, then, after 10 minutes, increase the heat and add the mushrooms. Fry quickly before adding the parsley and flour, followed by the gravy or stock. Stir continuously to prevent lumps from forming. Cook over a medium heat until the sauce boils, then add seasoning to taste and stir in the meat. Transfer to a deep pie dish.

Quarter the eggs and wrap each quarter in a piece of bacon. Arrange these on top of the meat. Cut the pâté (if used) into fingers and put them between the eggs.

Roll out the pastry into a sheet large enough to cover the pie with 5 cm/2 in to spare. Cut a 1 cm/½ in strip from round the edge of the pastry and press this around the edge of the dish. Brush the pastry rim with beaten egg and lift the pastry lid over the pie. Seal and flute the edges, then cut a small hole in the top of the pie to allow the steam to escape. Use any pastry trimmings to decorate the top of the pie. Glaze with beaten egg and bake in a hot oven (220c, 425f, gas 7) for 30 minutes. Reduce the temperature to moderately hot (190c, 375f, gas 5) and cook for a further 10 minutes. Serve hot or cold.

Festive Pheasant
Serves 4 to 6

Pheasants are usually plentiful around Christmas time, and cooking them this way not only keeps them moist and tender but it is also a change from making a

*rich sauce. Chicken can be used instead of pheasant if
you like.*

2 pheasants
75 g/3 oz butter
1 (425 g/15 oz) can pineapple cubes in natural juice
150 ml/¼ pint well-flavoured game stock
225 g/8 oz seedless grapes
salt and pepper
3 teaspoons arrowroot mixed with a little water
lemon juice to taste
1 orange, peeled and cut into segments

Wipe the pheasants inside and out with a damp cloth
and truss them neatly. Melt the butter in a heavy
flameproof casserole, then brown the pheasants, one
at a time, on all sides. Place both pheasants in the
casserole and add the pineapple cubes with their
juice, the stock and the grapes. Season with salt and
pepper. Cover and cook in a moderate oven (180c,
350F, gas 4) for 1 to 1½ hours or until tender. Transfer
the pheasants to a heated serving dish, remove any
string and keep hot.

Strain the sauce, reserving the fruit. Bring the liquid
to the boil and stir in the arrowroot mixture. Add
the lemon juice and adjust the seasoning. Stir in the
reserved fruit and orange segments. Pour a little sauce
over the birds; hand the rest separately.

Veal in Stilton Sauce
Serves 6

6 thin escalopes of veal, pork or turkey
75 g/3 oz butter
300 ml/½ pint soured cream
100 g/4 oz ripe Stilton cheese, crumbled
black pepper to taste

Trim the meat. Heat the butter in a large heavy-based
frying pan. Add the escalopes and fry for 1 to 2
minutes on each side, or until they are golden brown.

Remove the meat from the pan, transfer to a heated serving dish and keep hot.

Add the cream to the juices remaining in the pan and stir well over a low heat to dissolve any meat juices. Stir in the Stilton and season with black pepper, then pour this over the meat and serve with a salad.

Beef Loaf
Serves 6

1 kg/2 lb chuck steak, minced
4 tablespoons fresh breadcrumbs
½ red pepper, deseeded and finely chopped
1 large onion, grated
1 tablespoon tomato purée
½ teaspoon dried mixed herbs
salt and pepper
2 eggs, lightly beaten
FILLING
350 g/12 oz mashed potato
100 g/4 oz Cheddar cheese, grated
salt and pepper
TOPPING
75 g/3 oz cheese, sliced (optional)
Home-made Tomato Sauce (page 80)

Good for those meals when you have a mixture of children and adults. This beef roll is also delicious cold with chutney. Alternative filling:— Chopped spinach and cottage cheese, or mashed cooked carrots

In a large mixing bowl, combine the minced steak, breadcrumbs, chopped red pepper, onion, tomato purée, herbs and seasoning; mix well. Add the lightly beaten eggs and stir well until the mixture is thoroughly combined. For the filling, combine the mashed potato, grated cheese and seasoning until smooth.

Lay a sheet of greaseproof paper flat on a work surface and turn the meat mixture out on to it. Shape the meat into a flat rectangle of even thickness (about 1.5 cm/¾ in thick) and about 23 × 33 cm/9 × 13 in in size. Make sure the meat is thoroughly bound together. Pile the potato mixture down the middle of the meat, then carefully lift one edge of the greaseproof paper and fold the meat over the potato filling (it should come about halfway over the top). Now lift the opposite side and fold the meat over to completely enclose the potato. The greaseproof paper should lift off the meat quite easily: it should not stick. Roll the paper back slightly and pinch the join in the meat together quite securely. Pinch the meat at the ends of the roll to completely enclose the filling. Use the greaseproof paper to lift the meat on to a large baking tray or roasting tin, then carefully roll the loaf off the paper (on to the tin) so that the join in the meat is underneath. Check that the ends are well sealed: if the meat does not completely enclose the filling the potato will run out during cooking.

Bake in a moderate oven (160C, 325F, gas 3) for 1½ hours. Overlap the slices of cheese (if used) on top of the meat and bake for a further 15 minutes or until the cheese melts. Serve hot or cold, cut into slices. If serving hot, carefully lift the roll on to a serving dish and pour the Home-made Tomato Sauce over the top.

Beef Casserole with Walnuts
Serves 6 to 8

1 kg/2 lb lean chuck steak
600 ml/1 pint Guinness
4 large onions, thinly sliced
50 g/2 oz root ginger, peeled and chopped
4 tablespoon oil
1 bay leaf
1 teaspoon mixed spice
1 tablespoon flour
salt and pepper
75–100 g/3–4 oz walnut halves

I always add some slivers of lemon rind to casseroles for the last 15 minutes of cooking.

Cut the beef into large cubes and put them in a china, glass or earthenware bowl with the Guinness, sliced onions, finely chopped ginger, 1 tablespoon of the oil, the bay leaf and mixed spice. Mix well, then cover and leave to marinate in a cool place for 1 to 2 hours.

When ready to cook the casserole, remove the cubes of beef from the marinade and pat them dry on absorbent kitchen paper. Heat the remaining oil in a heavy flameproof casserole. Add the beef and brown thoroughly on all sides — you'll probably find that it is best to do this in several batches. Remove and set aside.

Strain the marinade, reserving the liquid and the vegetables. Add the onions and ginger to the oil in the casserole, and cook over low heat, stirring frequently, until soft and transparent. Stir in the flour, followed by the liquid from the marinade. Bring to the boil, stirring constantly, then add the bay leaf, the meat and its juices, salt and pepper and the walnuts. Stir gently, then cover and cook in a moderate oven (180c, 350f, gas 4) for 45 minutes. Stir gently, replace the cover and reduce the heat to 160c, 325f, gas 3. Cook for a further 45 minutes or until the meat is very tender. Stir gently and taste for seasoning before serving with Red Cabbage with Apples and Prunes (page 65) or Creamed Potatoes with Celeriac (page 62).

Beef with Peppers Casserole
Serves 8

This can be prepared earlier in the day or the day before and heated gently when required.

This is the type of recipe that doesn't need a starter — and it's perfect for those occasions when you're not quite sure if your guests will be on time. This casserole sits waiting quite happily. Follow it with fruit and cheese — or sorbet — and you will have a delicious but easy dinner.

225 g/8 oz streaky bacon, chopped small with scissors	
1 large onion, chopped	
1 dessertspoon dried oregano	
2 red peppers, deseeded and chopped	
4 carrots, cut in to strips	
1.3 kg/3 lb chuck steak, cut into 1½ inch pieces	
4 dessertspoons flour	
900 ml/1½ pints red wine	
900 ml/1½ pints beef stock	
2 dessertspoons tomato purée	
1½ dessertspoons butter	
225 g/8 oz mushrooms	
225 g/8 oz tiny onions, steamed until just tender	
salt and pepper	
1 tablespoon redcurrant jelly	

Sauté the bacon gently and drain on an absorbent paper towel. Into the bacon fat add the chopped onion, oregano, peppers and carrots and sauté for about 3 minutes. Remove and drain on paper towel. Add the meat and brown on all sides. Add the flour and stir well. Add wine, stock and tomato purée and stir till well blended.

Put the meat, vegetables and sauce into a large pot and cook in a moderately hot oven (180c, 350f, Gas 4) for about 2 hours or until the meat feels tender. Add mushrooms and tiny onions, season and stir in redcurrant jelly. Leave in the oven for about 10 minutes. Serve sprinkled with fresh parsley and croûtons, and with jacket potatoes or rice and a salad.

Family Beef Bourguignonne
Serves 6

1 kg / 2 lb lean chuck steak, cut into cubes
50 g / 2 oz flour
3 tablespoons oil
2 large onions, chopped
2 carrots, thinly sliced
2 cloves garlic, crushed
½ bottle red wine
bouquet garni
1 tablespoon chopped parsley
salt and pepper

I sometimes cut out shapes of puff pastry and bake them until golden, then arrange them on the beef just before serving.

Toss the meat in the flour until well covered. Heat the oil until very hot, then sauté the meat a few pieces at a time until brown. Transfer the pieces to an ovenproof casserole dish.

Fry the onions, carrots and garlic in the remaining fat. Add the wine, bouquet garni, parsley and seasoning. Stir well and pour over the meat. Cook in a moderate oven (160c, 325f, gas 3) for 3 hours.

Lamb Stuffed with Fruit
Serves 8

1 leg of lamb (about 2.5 kg / 5 lb in weight), boned and flattened
pinch of sea salt
225 g / 8 oz dried mixed fruit

| 50 g / 2 oz butter |
| 1 tablespoon chopped onion |
| 2 sticks celery, finely chopped |
| 25 g / 1 oz fresh breadcrumbs |
| 1 tablespoon juniper berries, crushed |
| 2 tablespoons redcurrant jelly |

with this I serve drained pear halves with a spoonful of red-currant or mint jelly in each half.

Sprinkle the lamb with coarse salt. Set aside 4 tablespoons of the mixed fruit. Melt the butter in a frying pan and sauté the onion and celery in it until soft, but not brown. Add the breadcrumbs and fruit and stir together until mixed. Spoon this filling over the flattened lamb, leaving a 1 cm/½ in border all round. Roll up, starting from the long side, and tie neatly in shape with string. Place the joint in a roasting tin, seam-side down and sprinkle the juniper berries on top.

Roast the lamb in a moderate oven (180c, 350f, gas 4) for 2 to 2½ hours. About 30 minutes before the end of the cooking time spread the redcurrant jelly over the meat. Make a gravy in the usual way, using the cooking juices, vegetable water and thickening if you like. Add the reserved fruit to the gravy.

Glazed Ham with Orange Sauce
Serves 8

| joint of middle or corner gammon (about 1.8 kg/4 lb in weight) |
| 1 large onion |
| 1 bay leaf |
| 6 peppercorns |
| 75 g / 3 oz soft brown sugar |
| 1 teaspoon dry mustard |
| cloves |
| ORANGE SAUCE |
| 2 tablespoons redcurrant or quince jelly |
| grated rind and juice of 3 oranges |
| grated rind and juice of 1 lemon |
| 2 teaspoons creamed horseradish |
| 1 teaspoon French mustard |
| 1 teaspoon vinegar |

Soak the gammon overnight in cold water. Drain the meat and put it in a large saucepan with cold water to cover; add the onion, bay leaf and peppercorns. Bring to the boil, skim the surface of the water and reduce the heat. Cover, then simmer for 1½ hours.

Remove the joint from the pan, peel off the skin and mark the fat into diamond shapes with a sharp knife. Reserve the stock, if you like, for making soup. Stand the gammon in a roasting tin. Mix the sugar and mustard together and press this over the fat. Press a clove into the corner of each diamond. Roast in a hot oven (220C, 425F, gas 7) for about 15 to 30 minutes or until the fat is crisp and golden.

Meanwhile, make the orange sauce. Melt the red-currant or quince jelly in a saucepan, add the fruit rind and juice and stir well. Stir in the horseradish, mustard and vinegar and heat through. This sweet and sour sauce can be served either hot or cold.

The bigger the ham, the better it is. This is an ideal dish for a lot of people.

Saturday Supper Chicken
Serves 6

1 chicken (about 1.5 kg/3½ lb in weight), boned (ask your butcher to do this)
STUFFING
1 large onion
50 g/2 oz butter
1 clove garlic
grated rind of 2 oranges
225 g/8 oz tomatoes
2 generous tablespoons chopped tarragon
175 g/6 oz buckwheat
300 ml/½ pint water
salt and pepper
50 g/2 oz fresh wholemeal breadcrumbs
a little orange juice
mayonnaise to serve

Lay the chicken flat on a large oiled roasting tin. Cook the onion in the butter with the garlic until soft but not browned. Add the orange rind and set aside.

Pour boiling water over the tomatoes and leave them for a minute. Drain and use a sharp knife to

Roast a chicken with plenty of rosemary or tarragon. Serve it hot with cold vinaigrette poured over at the last minute — sounds odd, tastes delicious!

slide off the skin. Chop the rest, discarding any bits of core. Stir the tomatoes and tarragon into the onion mixture.

Put the buckwheat in a saucepan with the water and add a little seasoning, then bring to the boil, cover and cook gently for about 10 minutes until the water has been absorbed. Remove from the heat and stir in the onion mixture with plenty of seasoning, the breadcrumbs and enough orange juice to bind the mixture together.

Use the stuffing to fill the chicken and sew it up neatly. Dot with butter and roast in a moderately hot oven (190c, 375f, gas 5) for about 1½ hours until the chicken is well cooked and tender. Serve hot, or cold with mayonnaise.

Summer Vegetable Lasagne
Serves 4 to 6

225 g/8 oz lasagne (use the type you prefer – wholemeal, green or the easy-cook one)
1 cauliflower, cooked
450 g/1 lb carrots
450 g/1 lb spinach
3 large onions
75 g/3 oz butter
bay leaf
1 clove garlic, crushed
225 g/8 oz cream cheese
salt and pepper
handful of fresh parsley, chopped
grated rind of 1 orange
freshly grated nutmeg
SAUCE
25 g/1 oz butter
25 g/1 oz plain flour
450 ml/¾ pint milk
100 g/4 oz matured Cheddar cheese, grated

Cook the lasagne in plenty of boiling salted water for about 15 minutes. Drain and rinse under cold water, then put the pieces to one side, laying them on absorbent kitchen paper.

For the fillings, steam the cauliflower until it is tender – about 10 minutes. Cook the carrots in boiling salted water for about 15 to 20 minutes, then drain thoroughly. Trim and shred the spinach, wash the leaves and shake off some of the water. Cook the spinach in the water which remains in the leaves, allowing about 3 to 5 minutes. Drain thoroughly.

Chop the onions and cook them in the butter with the bay leaf until they are soft. Add the garlic, cook for a further few minutes, then remove the bay leaf. Take off the heat. Purée the cauliflower, then beat in half the cream cheese, seasoning and chopped parsley. Add about a third of the cooked onion.

Purée the carrots, beat in the remaining cream cheese with the orange rind, seasoning and some more parsley. Stir about half the remaining onion into the carrot purée.

You can purée the spinach or leave the leaves whole – whichever you prefer. However, add seasoning and some nutmeg with the remaining onion and stir well, then set aside.

To make the sauce, melt the butter in a saucepan, add the flour and blend well for a minute before stirring in the milk. Bring to the boil and cook for 3 minutes before adding seasoning to taste and most of the cheese. Stir until the cheese melts, then remove the pan from the heat.

Layer the cooked lasagne with the three different vegetables, keeping each type separate. Pour the sauce over the top and sprinkle with the remaining cheese, then bake in a moderate oven (180c, 350f, gas 4) for 30 to 35 minutes, or until golden and bubbling.

Speedy Pasta
Serves 6

450 g / 1 lb fresh thin noodles
300 ml / ½ pint single cream
50 g / 2 oz Parmesan or Cheddar cheese, grated
100 g / 4 oz Gorgonzola cheese, crumbled
100 g / 4 oz toasted pine nuts
extra cheese to serve

Cook the pasta in boiling salted water for 3 to 4 minutes. Warm the cream with the cheese over a gentle heat, then add the pine nuts. Drain the pasta and put it in a serving dish, then pour the sauce over and serve sprinkled with extra cheese.

Tuna Cannelloni
Serves 4

12 cannelloni tubes
50 g/2 oz butter
50 g/2 oz flour
600 ml/1 pint milk
salt and pepper
2 teaspoons dried oregano
some chopped parsley
50 g/2 oz Cheddar cheese, grated
25 g/1 oz Parmesan cheese, grated
2 (198 g/7 oz) cans tuna in brine, drained
a few spring onions, chopped
50 g/2 oz button mushrooms, chopped
juice of 1 lemon
TOPPING
cupful of breadcrumbs
a little extra Parmesan cheese, grated

Cook the cannelloni tubes in plenty of boiling salted water until they are tender but not too soft. (Or use the type which doesn't need pre-cooking.) Drain thoroughly and rinse under cold water, then set aside on a double-thick piece of absorbent kitchen paper.

Melt the butter in a saucepan. Add the flour, blend well and pour in the milk, still stirring. Bring to the boil, stirring all the time, then add seasoning, the herbs and both lots of cheese. Stir over a low heat until the cheese melts, then remove from the heat.

Flake the tuna into a bowl, add the onions and mushrooms with the lemon juice and seasoning. Add about a quarter of the sauce to bind the mixture.

Fill the drained cannelloni with the tuna mixture, then put them in a buttered ovenproof dish and pour the rest of the sauce over the top. Sprinkle with the breadcrumbs and cheese for topping and bake in a moderately hot oven (180C, 350F, gas 4) for 30 minutes, or until the top is nicely browned and crisp.

Spinach Cannelloni
Serves 4

12 cannelloni tubes (the type which doesn't need pre-cooking)
STUFFING
50 g/2 oz butter
1 (225 g/8 oz) packet frozen chopped spinach, defrosted and squeezed dry
225 g/8 oz cottage cheese
1 egg, beaten
salt and pepper
grated nutmeg
50 g/2 oz Cheddar cheese, grated
SAUCE
50 g/2 oz butter
50 g/2 oz flour
600 ml/1 pint milk
75 g/3 oz Cheddar cheese, grated
TOPPING
50 g/2 oz fresh breadcrumbs
50 g/2 oz Cheddar cheese, grated

Don't stuff this type of pasta too long before you are going to cook it.

Mix all the stuffing ingredients together and carefully fill the cannelloni tubes. Lay in a greased ovenproof dish.

For the sauce, melt the butter and stir in the flour. Pour in the milk, bring to the boil and add seasoning. Cook for 2 to 3 minutes and stir in the cheese.

Pour the sauce over the cannelloni and sprinkle with the topping. Bake in a moderate oven (180C, 350F, gas 4) until brown and bubbly.

Baked Mullet
Serves 4

4 red mullet
juice of 1 lemon
salt and pepper

4 tablespoons chopped chives
100 g / 4 oz butter
300 ml / ½ pint dry white wine
sprigs of dill, to garnish

A delicious alternative to this is baked mackerel. Roll the mackerel in oatmeal and grated apple. Mix together, then bake in a medium to hot oven for about 10 minutes.

Ask the fishmonger to clean the mullet for you — he may descale them too but if not then do this by scraping off the scales from the tail end towards head end. Hold the fish in the sink because the scales will fly off everywhere.

Wash and dry the mullet, then sprinkle them inside and out with the lemon juice. Season to taste and sprinkle the chives in the fish. Place each mullet on a piece of foil, dot with some of the butter (you should have at least half the quantity left) and pack tightly. Put the packages on a roasting tin and bake in a moderate oven (180c, 350f, gas 4) for about 30 minutes.

Pour the wine into a saucepan and bring to the boil. Add all the cooking juices from each package and put the fish on warmed plates; keep hot. Add the remaining butter to the wine and boil hard until the liquid has reduced to one-third of its original quantity. Taste and add seasoning, then pour over the fish. Garnish with dill and serve.

Cabbage Pie
Serves 6 to 8

7 g / ¼ oz butter
about 12 (or more) Savoy cabbage leaves (depending on size)
675 g / 1½ lb cooked vegetables (a mixture of as many of the following as you wish: sliced carrots, sliced onions, sliced leeks, diced parsnips, sliced or diced courgettes, roughly chopped spinach, sliced or chopped cabbage, whole, diced or sliced green or runner beans, diced or sliced potatoes, halved Brussels sprouts, peas, sliced green, red or yellow peppers, sliced aubergines and sliced mushrooms)
salt and pepper
4 eggs, lightly beaten

100 g/4 oz Cheddar cheese, grated
200 ml/7 fl oz single cream
2 tablespoons chopped parsley or chives

Butter a 25 cm/10 in quiche dish. Remove and discard the hard stalk from the Savoy cabbage leaves, then blanch them in boiling salted water for about 3 minutes or until just tender. Drain, rinse with cold water, then drain again thoroughly. Use these cabbage leaves to line the quiche dish, placing them so that they overlap the sides of the dish.

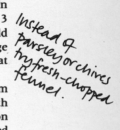

Instead of parsley or chives try fresh-chopped fennel.

Put the cooked vegetables in a bowl and mix them thoroughly with seasoning to taste. Mix the eggs with the cheese and cream, stir in half the herbs and season to taste. Spoon the vegetable mixture into the lined quiche dish and pour over the egg mixture. Fold the cabbage leaves over the filling, using more cabbage leaves if necessary to completely cover the filling. Bake in a moderately hot oven (190c, 375f, gas 5) for about 30 minutes, or until golden and set. Sprinkle with the remaining herbs and serve hot, from the dish, or turn out. Served cold, this tastes equally as good.

Chicken and Sage Terrine
Serves 6 to 8

This is great for busy weekends because it is made at least a day in advance or it freezes well.

1 large onion, finely chopped
2 large cloves garlic, crushed
50 g/2 oz butter
several sprigs of fresh sage, chopped
675 g/1½ lb uncooked boneless chicken breast
a handful of parsley, chopped
salt and pepper
several sprigs of thyme
grated rind of 1 large lemon
4 tablespoons brandy
1 small egg, beaten
50 g/2 oz breadcrumbs
4 bay leaves
100 g/4 oz button mushrooms, thinly sliced

Sauté the onion with the garlic in the butter until soft but not browned. Add the sage to the onion, stir well and transfer to a bowl.

Mince the chicken (or whizz it up in a food processor to chop it very finely) and add to the onion mixture with the parsley, plenty of seasoning, the leaves from the thyme, lemon rind, brandy and egg. Stir in the breadcrumbs.

Grease a 1 kg/2 lb loaf tin, dish or terrine. Line the base with greaseproof paper and grease it well. Arrange the bay leaves in the tin.

Put half the chicken mixture into the tin and press it down lightly. Spoon the mushrooms on top and season to taste. Add the remaining chicken mixture, pressing down well. Cover with cooking foil or greaseproof paper and stand in a roasting tin half filled with boiling water. Cook in a moderate oven (180c, 350f, gas 4) for 2 hours.

Weight the cooked terrine down with a double thickness of cooking foil and something heavy (a heavy weight from scales or a brick wrapped in greaseproof paper). When cold, chill overnight, then turn out and remove the greaseproof paper. Serve sliced.

Sole with Asparagus
Serves 3

This is good for a dinner party because you can prepare the fish and prepare the sauce — then combine and cook when you are ready.

12 aparagus spears	
6 sole fillets, skinned	
salt and pepper	
zest of a lemon	
50 g/2 oz butter	
4 tablespoons lemon juice	
8 spring onions, finely chopped	
1 teaspoon Dijon mustard	

Cut the asparagus to about 7.5 cm/3 in. Steam until just tender. Lay out the sole, skinned side up. Sprinkle with salt, pepper and lemon zest. Place 2 asparagus spears on each sole fillet and roll up. Place seam side down in buttered baking dish.

Melt the butter, add the lemon juice, spring onions and mustard, and pour over the fish. Bake in a hot oven (200c, 400F, gas 6) for about 15 minutes until the fish flakes.

Red Flannel Hash
Serves 4 to 6

1 dessertspoon butter
1 tablespoon oil
about 150 g/6 oz corned beef, chopped
about 350 g/12 oz chopped cooked boiled potatoes
1 large onion, peeled and chopped
100 g/4 oz beetroot, chopped

Heat the butter and oil in a frying pan. Fold all the remaining ingredients together, spread them into pan and brown slowly. When a crust has formed, turn over and brown the other side. Serve with creamed horseradish.

Fish Loaf
Serves 4 to 6

2 eggs, separated
225 g/8 oz flaked fish
150 g/6 oz breadcrumbs
½ green and ½ red pepper, deseeded and finely chopped and mixed together
1 dessertspoon lemon juice
150 ml/¼ pint milk
50 g/2 oz chopped walnuts
1 dessertspoon chopped parsley
salt and pepper

Beat the egg yolks in a bowl. Add all the remaining ingredients and lastly fold in the beaten egg whites. Bake in a greased loaf tin in a moderately hot oven (190c, 375F, gas 5) for about 40 minutes.

Spiced Halibut
Serves 4

about 900 g/2 lb halibut, skinned and breaded
SAUCE
½ onion, finely chopped
½ green pepper, deseeded and finely chopped
1 clove garlic, finely chopped
2.5 cm/1 in piece of fresh root ginger, finely chopped
1 stick celery, finely chopped
4 whole tomatoes (tinned are best), chopped
2 tablespoons lemon juice
150 ml/¼ pint white wine
225 g/8 oz mushrooms, thinly sliced
4 dessertspoons soy sauce
2 dessertspoons oil
salt and pepper to taste

First make the sauce. Heat the oil. Add the onion, pepper, garlic, ginger and celery and cook gently until softened. Add the tomatoes, lemon juice and wine. Simmer for about 5 minutes. Add the mushrooms and leave to cook. Season to taste.

Place the halibut in an ovenproof serving dish and pour over the sauce. Bake in a moderately hot oven (190c, 375f, gas 5) for about 10 to 15 minutes or until the fish flakes easily.

Side Effects

Fresh vegetables, steamed and served with a sprinkling of herbs, a knob of butter, or perhaps just a squeeze of lemon, are unbeatable, and would always be my first choice. But there are times when you might want to dress them up a little. So here are a few ideas. If your main course is rich, serve a simple vegetable or green salad. With cold meats, go to town on the side effects.

Vegetable Ideas

Creamed Potatoes with Celeriac Cook together, in salted simmering water, an equal quantity of potatoes and celeriac (peeled and cut into even-sized pieces). When the vegetables are tender, drain and mash them together until smooth. Beat in a little hot milk and a large knob of butter with salt and pepper to taste. Add a little freshly grated nutmeg and serve immediately.

Turnip Purée Cook the turnip, peeled and cut into even-sized pieces, in salted simmering water until tender. Drain and mash thoroughly, then beat in a little butter and cream (or top of the milk). Add seasoning to taste and some chopped fresh chives or parsley.

Carrot Purée Purée cooked carrots in a food processor or mash well. Add a knob of butter or a spoonful of cream. Just before serving, add a grated raw eating apple.

Spinach and Pear Purée Peel, core and dice two ripe pears. Put them in a saucepan with a large knob of butter and cook gently for a few minutes. Add 450 g / 1 lb frozen leaf spinach and cook gently until thawed. Boil rapidly until the excess liquid has evaporated, then purée the mixture in a liquidiser or food processor. Season with salt, pepper and a little grated nutmeg, add a knob of butter and serve.

Roast Parsnips Peel and quarter as many parsnips as you need. Blanch the vegetables in boiling salted water for 1 minute, then drain them and dust the pieces with a little flour. Roast the parsnips with a joint or bird, in a roasting tin, adding a little oil if necessary. The vegetables should take about 1 hour to cook (depending on the oven temperature). Turn and baste the parsnips occasionally; when cooked they should be brown and crisp.

Braised Vegetables These can be cooked in the oven at the same time as the meat. To braise chicory or leeks, trim and blanch the vegetables in boiling salted water for 1 minute. Melt 40 g / 1½ oz butter in a flameproof casserole, then add a couple of sliced onions, a chopped carrot and a sliced stick of celery. Cook gently for about 15 minutes, then add a little fresh thyme, a few sprigs of parsley and

a bay leaf. Pour in enough stock
the vegetables and add seasoning to
or celery on top and cover the casserole,
moderate oven (180C, 350F, gas 4) for about
minutes, or until tender. Transfer the cooked ve
to a heated serving dish. Strain and thicken the coo
liquid if you like, then pour it over the vegetables. Ser
immediately.

Sautéed Turnips and Apples Sauté thinly sliced
turnips in butter, then add two thinly sliced apples, a few
chopped spring onions and some chopped walnuts and
parsley. Sauté together briefly.

Carrots Dill gives plain steamed carrots a delightful zest.

Grilled Courgettes Place small thinnish courgettes,
cut in half lengthways, brushed with oil and sprinkled
with salt and pepper, under the grill. When they start to
change colour, sprinkle with grated Parmesan and grill
till golden.

Grilled Fennel Trim fennel bulbs and cut them into long
slices. Place them on baking sheets, spoon over a little
olive oil, salt and pepper. Grill for about 5 minutes, quite
a distance from the heat. Then move around, and place
them closer to the grill and cook for a further 5 minutes.
(You can make this more interesting by removing the
cooked fennel, sprinkling it with Parmesan cheese, then
adding thin slivers of ham and returning it to the grill for
a few minutes.)

Roast Peppers The easiest way to roast peppers is to
put them in the oven, or under the grill, until the skin
is blistered and blackened. Remove (with tongs), put in
a plastic bag, close and leave to cool. You can peel and
deseed them reasonably easily.

...r water to just cover
...ste. Lay the leeks
...then cook in a
...30 to 40
...etables
...king
...

...ly chopped

...d and cut into strips
...eded and cut into strips
...seeded and cut into strips
...

...sh thyme
...parsley

Have it hot or cold – delicious – as a supper dish with sliced mozzarella cheese melted on top and chunks of high hot bread.

Wipe... ...m off their stalks and cut them into fingers. ... colander, sprinkle with salt and set aside for 30 minutes. Pat them dry with absorbent kitchen paper.

Heat a little of the oil in a frying pan. Add the aubergines and sauté briefly over high heat until golden brown. Remove and drain on absorbent kitchen paper. Add a little more oil and fry all the remaining vegetables individually in the same way. Season each with a little salt, pepper and coriander. Mix with the garlic in an ovenproof casserole, sprinkling in the thyme. Cover and bake in a moderately hot oven (190c, 375f, gas 5) for 30 to 35 minutes or until tender. Sprinkle with the parsley before serving either hot or cold.

Red Cabbage with Apples and Prunes
Serves 4 to 6

1 small red cabbage
a large handful of prunes, stoned
2 apples, peeled and chopped
a scant tablespoon brown sugar
175 ml/6 fl oz cider vinegar

Remove the hard central core, then chop or shred the red cabbage and put it into a large saucepan with the

rest of the ingredients. Cook, covered, over a low heat, stirring from time to time, until the cabbage is tender – about 40 minutes.
Note: This dish reheats very well.

Carrot Pudding
Serves 4 to 6

675 g / 1½ lb carrots, peeled and sliced
900 ml / 1½ pints chicken stock
1 teaspoon sugar
2 teaspoons oil
knob of butter
1 onion, finely chopped
4 eggs, lightly beaten
225 g / 8 oz Cheddar or Gruyère cheese, grated
50 g / 2 oz fresh breadcrumbs
2 teaspoons chopped chives or parsley

Served with herb bread, this is nice as a first course.

Cook the carrots in the chicken stock until tender, then set aside to cool. When cool add the sugar and purée the mixture in a liquidiser.

In another saucepan, heat the oil and butter, then add the onion and cook gently until soft. Stir the cooked onion into the carrot purée with the lightly beaten eggs. Fold in 175 g / 6 oz of the cheese and season to taste. Pour the carrot mixture into a lightly buttered shallow ovenproof dish. Sprinkle with the rest of the cheese, breadcrumbs and herbs.

Cook in a moderate oven (180C, 350F, gas 4) for 50 to 60 minutes or until the pudding is set. Serve immediately.

Beetroot Mashed Potatoes
Serves 6 to 8

1 kg / 2 lb potatoes
4 tablespoons milk
50 g / 2 oz butter
salt and pepper
100 g / 4 oz uncooked beetroot

This may sound odd but the taste is lovely, and so is the colour: it cheers up bangers and mash.

Peel the potatoes and cut them into even-sized pieces. Cook them in simmering salted water until tender, then mash the drained potatoes with the milk, butter, salt and pepper. Set aside and keep hot.

Wash, peel and grate the beetroot and add it to the mashed potato. Stir thoroughly until the potatoes have absorbed all the colour and the beetroot is evenly distributed. Serve immediately. This is excellent with plain roast meat, cold cooked chicken or turkey.

Alternative ideas for mashed potato:

Mix grated raw carrot, toasted flaked almonds, or chopped spring onions into the potatoes before serving.

Moulded Sweet and Sour Rice
Serves 4 to 6

225 g/8 oz brown (or white) long-grain rice
900 ml/1½ pints water
100 g/4 oz nuts, chopped (walnuts, peanuts, Brazils or pine nuts)
50 g/2 oz dried apricots, chopped
handful of sultanas
1 yellow pepper, deseeded and chopped
1 red pepper, deseeded and chopped
a few radishes, thinly sliced
bunch of spring onions, chopped
100 g/4 oz sweetcorn
plenty of chopped herbs (parsley, chives, tarragon or basil, all taste good)
salt and pepper
watercress, iceberg lettuce or alfalfa sprouts to serve
DRESSING
4 tablespoons sunflower oil
1 tablespoon cider vinegar
squeeze of lemon juice
salt and pepper
1 teaspoon honey
large pinch of mustard powder

Try this recipe with wild rice.

Put the rice and water in a saucepan, boil and cook until the rice is just tender. Drain well. Add all the remaining ingredients.

Shake all the ingredients for the dressing in a

screw-top jar. Stir in the dressing while the rice is still warm. Press into a 1.4 litre/2½ pint ring mould or basin. Leave overnight or for a few hours. Turn out on to a large flat dish. Decorate with watercress, Iceberg lettuce or alfalfa sprouts (or all of these). Sprinkle with a little salad dressing.

Serve this with any cold meats or chicken or ham. Add a large green salad and you have an easy (prepared ahead) minimum-time-in-the-kitchen lunch.

Vegetable Terrine
Serves 8

This dish sounds complicated, but it's well worth the extra effort.

CARROT MIXTURE

225 g/8 oz carrots, peeled and cut into small pieces

2 eggs yolks

2 tablespoons double cream

salt and pepper

SPINACH MIXTURE

450 g/1 lb frozen chopped spinach, thawed

2 tablespoons double cream

2 egg yolks

salt and pepper

pinch of nutmeg

15 g/½ oz flour

CAULIFLOWER MIXTURE

225 g/8 oz cauliflower, cut into small pieces

2 tablespoons double cream

2 egg yolks

salt and pepper

3 egg whites (divided between all the above
 mixtures)

HOLLANDAISE SAUCE

2 tablespoons white wine vinegar

3 tablespoons lemon juice

6 eggs yolks

salt and pepper

350 g/12 oz unsalted butter, melted

2 tablespoons chopped fresh herbs

1 tomato, peeled and diced

First, prepare the carrot mixture: purée the uncooked carrots in a food processor. Then blend with the egg yolks and cream, adding seasoning to taste. For the spinach mixture, you must first squeeze all the liquid from the chopped spinach. Purée the spinach with the cream, egg yolks, seasoning, nutmeg and flour. Finally, purée the uncooked cauliflower, then blend in the cream, egg yolks and seasoning.

Whisk the egg whites until they stand in stiff peaks, then divide them equally between the three mixtures and fold in gently using a metal spoon. Line and grease a 1 kg/2 lb loaf tin. Spread the spinach mixture in the base of the tin and smooth over the top to give an even layer. Next spoon the cauliflower mixture on top and smooth the top. Lastly top with the carrot mixture. Cover with greased cooking foil and stand the tin in a roasting tin half filled with hot water. Bake in a moderate oven (160C, 325F, gas 3) for 2½ hours, or until set. Cool slightly in the tin before turning out on to a heated serving dish.

Towards the end of the cooking time make the sauce: bring the vinegar and lemon juice to the boil. Put the egg yolks in a liquidiser or food processor with a little seasoning. Blend briefly, then gradually pour in the hot vinegar mixture followed by the melted butter. Do not pour the butter in too quickly or the sauce will curdle. Transfer the sauce to a warmed sauce boat or dish, stir in the herbs and diced tomato, and adjust the seasoning if necessary. Serve the sauce to accompany the terrine.

Yams in Orange Shells
Serves 6

Try this American idea – sweet potatoes or yams in orange shells. Topped with marshmallows, these can be prepared in advance, then heated in the oven until the marshmallow is browned.

When making fresh orange juice, put the orange shells in the freezer for later use in this sort of recipe.

1 kg/2 lb yams or sweet potatoes
2 tablespoons single cream
50 g/2 oz butter
salt and pepper

| 6 scooped-out oranges |
| a few small white marshmallows (optional) |

Scrub and bake the yams or sweet potatoes in the oven until soft. Scoop the vegetables out of the shells and mash with the cream and butter, salt and pepper. Spoon this mixture into the orange shells, and serve right away as they are, or stand them in an ovenproof dish and top with marshmallows, then bake in a moderate oven (180c, 350f, gas 4) for 10 to 15 minutes or until the marshmallow begins to brown.

Vegetable Pie
Serves 6

This is particularly useful for a vegetarian meal. Try different combinations of vegetables – you can't go wrong!

| 2 large onions, sliced |
| 1 tablespoon oil |
| 4 carrots, sliced |
| 3 courgettes, sliced |
| 1 cauliflower, divided into florets |
| salt and pepper |
| 75 g/3 oz plain flour |
| 75 g/3 oz butter |
| 900 ml/1½ pints milk |
| 1 tablespoon chopped fresh herbs (choose your favourite herbs or tarragon is delicious) |
| 100 g/4 oz cooked butter beans |
| 1 (215 g/7½ oz) packet frozen puff pastry, thawed |
| beaten egg to glaze |

Let yourself be carried away with the pastry decorations for this pie — flowers, leaves, hearts, initials or a guest's name.

Sauté the onions in the oil until just soft. Drain on absorbent kitchen paper and set aside. Cook the prepared vegetables separately in salted simmering water for 10 minutes, or until tender but still crisp.

Meanwhile make the sauce: combine the flour, butter and milk together in a saucepan. Bring to the boil, whisking continuously, season, add the herbs and remove from the heat.

Drain the vegetables and arrange them (with the onions) in layers in a pie dish with the butter beans.

Pour the sauce over the vegetables. Roll the pastry out into a piece large enough to cover the pie with 5 cm/2 in to spare. Cut a narrow strip from round the pastry and press this on the rim of the dish; brush with beaten egg. Lift the lid over the pie, seal and flute the edges, then glaze the top. Bake in a moderately hot oven (190C, 375F, gas 5) for 30 minutes. Serve hot.

Parsnip Loaf

Makes 1
large loaf

Nice with home-made soup.

15 g/½ oz dried yeast
scant 300 ml/½ pint tepid water
1 teaspoon sugar
450 g/1 lb strong plain flour (or half plain, half wholemeal)
2 teaspoons salt
1 onion, finely chopped
100 g/4 oz Gruyère, grated
225 g/8 oz parsnips, cooked and mashed with a large knob of butter
handful of sesame seeds to sprinkle on top

Sprinkle the yeast over the tepid water. Stir in the sugar, then leave in a warm place until frothy.

Put the flour and salt in a bowl, then add the onion and cheese and mix well. Make a well in the middle, add the parsnips and stir in the yeast liquid, then mix in the flour to make a dough. Knead thoroughly for about 10 minutes. You can do this in a food mixer or food processor.

Shape the dough into a thick round loaf and put it on a greased baking tray. Cover with oiled cling film, leave in a warm place until doubled in size, then cut a cross in the top. Brush with a little water and sprinkle with the sesame seeds before baking in a hot oven (230C, 450F, gas 8) for about 40 minutes. When the loaf is cooked it will sound hollow when you tap the bottom. Leave to cool on a wire rack.

Pasta Salad
Serves 4 to 6

225 g/8 oz pasta shells, shapes or twists

150 ml/¼ pint mayonnaise

2 or 3 sticks celery, chopped

50 g/2 oz walnut pieces

black pepper

¼ teaspoon dried mixed herbs (or to taste)

lettuce leaves to serve

Instead of mayonnaise try a vinaigrette made with walnut oil.

Cook the pasta in plenty of simmering salted water for 10 to 12 minutes or until just tender, drain and cool.

Put the pasta into a serving dish, pour over the mayonnaise and mix well until the pasta is evenly coated. Add the celery and walnuts and again mix well. Finally, season with black pepper and mixed herbs.

Cover and chill until required, and serve in a bowl lined with lettuce leaves.

Sweet Pea Tart
Serves 4 to 6

If you are lucky enough to tire of fresh young peas out of the garden try this.

275 g/10 oz wholemeal flour

salt and pepper

228 g/8 oz butter or sunflower margarine

450 g/1 lb cooked peas

chopped mint

large bunch of spring onions, chopped

300 ml/½ pint single cream

3 large eggs, beaten

Put the flour in a bowl and add a generous pinch of salt, then rub in the butter or margarine and mix in only just enough cold water to make the pastry bind together. Alternatively, use a food processor.

Roll out the pastry and use to line a fairly deep 25 cm/10 in flan dish. Prick the base all over with a fork and put a sheet of greaseproof paper in the flan. Sprinkle in some dried peas or beans and bake the pastry case in a moderately hot oven (200C, 400F, gas 6) for 15 minutes.

Remove the paper and beans, then put the cooked peas in the flan. Sprinkle with mint and the spring onions. Beat the cream into the eggs, adding plenty of seasoning. Pour this over the filling and bake in a moderate oven (180c, 350f, gas 4) for 30 minutes or until set and lightly browned on top. Serve hot or cold.

Note: I like to serve this with mange-tout salad.

Caesar Salad
Serves 8

1 clove garlic, finely chopped
200 ml/8 fl oz olive oil
100 g/4 oz white bread, cubed
75 g/3 oz butter
2 eggs
2 cos lettuce, washed and torn into pieces
salt and pepper
juice of 1 lemon
6–8 anchovy fillets
100 g/4 oz fresh Parmesan cheese, grated

You probably have your favourite version of Caesar Salad. This one is V. Good.

Mix the garlic with 100 ml/4 fl oz of the olive oil a few hours before you are going to serve the salad. Sauté the cubes of bread in the butter until brown and crunchy, drain these croûtons and put aside.

Boil the eggs for exactly 1 minute. Cool. Strain the olive oil and mix it with the remaining unflavoured oil. Put the lettuce in a bowl, add seasoning and the oil and toss well. Break in the eggs, and the lemon juice, then toss again. Finally, add the anchovies, cheese and croûtons and toss carefully. Serve immediately.

Artist's Salad
Serves 6

1 bunch watercress, finely chopped
1 bunch spring onions, chopped
2 large carrots, grated
50 g/2 oz cheese, chopped
1 large uncooked beetroot, grated
2 large tomatoes, chopped
2 or 3 sticks celery, chopped

6 rindless rashers bacon, fried until crisp and crumbled

chopped parsley

florets of cauliflower

2 slices wholemeal bread, cut into squares and fried in butter

2 hard-boiled eggs, chopped

450 g / 1 lb cooked chicken or turkey, cut into neat squares

1 Iceberg lettuce, cut into chunks

DRESSING

150 ml / ¼ pint soured cream

150 ml / ¼ pint mayonnaise or your favourite vinaigrette

this can be served as a main course — and is great as part of a buffet-style meal.

Use a large, shallow salad bowl or platter. Arrange the salad ingredients in separate piles, according to the best colour effect — like an artist's palette. Mix the ingredients for the dressing and serve this separately. Toss the ingredients in the dressing only just before serving. Serve with French bread.

Minted Carrot Salad
Serves 4

2 tablespoons vegetable oil

1 tablespoon lemon juice or orange juice

a few mint leaves, chopped

salt and pepper

450 g / 1 lb large carrots, grated

sesame seeds, toasted

mint, to garnish

Mix the oil with the lemon or orange juice, the chopped mint and a little salt and pepper. Toss the carrots in this mixture. Cover and chill for an hour for the flavours to blend. Toss again, sprinkle with sesame seeds and garnish with a few sprigs of mint.
Note: For a stronger flavoured salad, replace the vegetable oil with olive oil, and add a couple of crushed cloves of garlic with a little grated lemon or orange rind.

Brown Rice Salad
Serves 6

1.15 litres/2 pints water
1 teaspoon salt
350 g/12 oz brown rice
2 large carrots, grated
12 spring onions, chopped
2 tablespoons chopped chives
2 tablespoons chopped parsley
100 g/4 oz white cabbage, grated
½ cucumber, chopped
about 6 tablespoons salad dressing of your choice
1 lettuce heart, broken into leaves
GARNISH
sprigs of watercress
tomato wedges

Bring the water and salt to the boil. Add the rice and cook for 30 to 40 minutes or until the grains are just tender, then drain thoroughly.

While the rice is still warm, mix in the grated carrots, spring onions, chives, parsley, cabbage and cucumber. Pour the salad dressing over and toss well. Press into a 1.15 litre/2 pint ring mould or pudding basin and leave to cool.

Arrange the lettuce heart on a serving platter. Invert the ring mould or basin on to the platter and lift the container off to serve the rice. Garnish before serving.

Watercress and Orange Salad with Pecan Nuts
Serves 4 to 6

6 oranges
2 large bunches watercress, trimmed and rinsed
100 g/4 oz pecans
DRESSING
the reserved juice from the oranges (see below)
4 tablespoons walnut or olive oil
1 tablespoon sherry or wine vinegar
¼ teaspoon mustard powder
salt and pepper

Peel and slice the oranges into rounds, keeping the juice for the dressing, then cut these slices in half. Mix the watercress, oranges and pecans.

Mix all the ingredients for the dressing and taste for seasoning; pour over the salad and toss well to mix. Serve immediately.

Pineapple, Pepper and Cottage Cheese Salad
Serves 4

The combination of pineapple, nuts and cottage cheese, makes an excellent accompaniment to a simple grilled meat dish. This salad can even be served as a pudding, or as lunch for the weight watchers.

1 ripe pineapple
225 g/8 oz cottage cheese
50 g/2 oz salted cashew nuts
2 sticks celery, finely chopped
1 green pepper, deseeded and finely chopped

Cut the pineapple in half lengthways. Cut out the flesh, remove the core and chop the fruit into chunks. Reserve the pineapple shell. Mix the pineapple chunks with the cottage cheese, cashew nuts, chopped celery and green pepper. Mix well and chill until required.

Spoon the salad into the reserved fruit shells and serve on a bed of lettuce, garnished, if you wish, with extra pepper slices.

Warm Spinach Salad
Serves 6

450 g/1 lb tender young spinach
bunch of spring onions, finely chopped
½ clove garlic
1 tablespoon salad oil
3 rindless rashers bacon
1 tablespoon sugar
1 tablespoon tarragon vinegar
1 tablespoon red wine vinegar
1 egg
salt and pepper

Wash and dry the spinach, tear it into small pieces and transfer to a salad bowl; add the spring onions. Mash the garlic into the oil and leave to stand, whilst preparing the rest of the salad. Dry-fry the bacon gently until very crisp, drain, crumble and add it to the spinach. Strain the garlic from the oil and pour the oil over the salad.

Whisk the sugar, vinegars, egg and seasoning together, pour into the bacon fat remaining in the pan and stir gently for a few seconds over a low heat until the egg mixture has thickened slightly.

Pour over the spinach and toss the salad so that all the ingredients are evenly combined. Serve immediately.

Red and Green Tomato Salad
Serves 4

450 g/1 lb each red and green tomatoes
1 small onion, chopped
1 teaspoon caster sugar
2 tablespoons cider vinegar
6 tablespoons olive oil
bunch of parsley, chopped
a few sprigs of mint
salt and pepper
1 (50 g/2 oz) can anchovies, chopped (optional)
chopped basil, to garnish

Cut the tomatoes into slices, keeping both types separate. Arrange them in rings on a platter, then sprinkle with the onion. Mix all the remaining ingredients in a screw-topped jar and shake well. Pour this over the salad and leave to marinate in a cool place (not the refrigerator) for about an hour. Serve cool but not chilled. Garnish with chopped basil.

Another way of using up tomatoes: lay thick slices of red and green tomatoes in a lightly buttered dish. Season with salt and pepper, and a teaspoon of sugar. Pour over some cream and sprinkle with grated Cheddar cheese. Bake in the oven until the cheese is just turning brown.

Tuna and Olive Salad
Serves 6

Served with crusty bread and its own tangy dressing this salad takes only minutes to prepare.

3 (198 g/7 oz) cans tuna in oil
2 green or yellow peppers
4 hard-boiled eggs
bunch of spring onions, chopped
50 g/2 oz black olives, stoned
4 tablespoons chopped parsley
vinaigrette dressing

Drain and flake the tuna. Cut the stalk ends off the peppers, remove any seeds and pith, then thinly slice. Chop the eggs then combine with the tuna, peppers, spring onions, black olives and parsley.

Keep the salad and dressing separate, covered with cling film or packed in a container in the refrigerator or chiller box. Dress the salad just before serving.

Black Bean Salad
Serves 4 to 6

2 cups black beans (or any other beans of your choice), soaked overnight and drained
1 red pepper, roasted and cut into thin strips
1 red onion, finely sliced
DRESSING
2 tablespoons sunflower oil
2 tablespoons walnut oil
1 tablespoon cider vinegar
salt and black pepper
1 teaspoon balsamic vinegar
chopped chives or parsley or oregano

Simmer the beans in plenty of water for about an hour until just soft. Leave to cool. To make the dressing, whizz the oils, vinegar, seasonings and herbs in a liquidiser or food processor until well mixed. Add the pepper and onion to the salad. Pour the dressing over the beans. Chill before serving.

Beetroot Salad
Serves 6

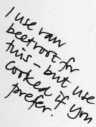

I use raw beetroot for this – but use cooked if you prefer.

1 crisp Iceberg lettuce
450 g / 1 lb beetroot
grated rind and juice of 1 lemon
celery salt and pepper
6 tablespoons olive oil
pinch of sugar
150 ml / ¼ pint soured cream
bunch of chives, chopped

Put the sliced lettuce on a serving dish. Peel and grate the beetroot, put in a bowl and toss in the lemon rind and juice, celery salt and pepper to taste, oil and sugar. Pile the beetroot on top of the lettuce. Pour the soured cream over and top with the chives.

Dressing the Salad

Everyone has a favourite vinaigrette dressing; mine is equal quantities of walnut oil and best quality olive oil, with a dash of balsamic vinegar and a dash of tarragon vinegar, 1 teaspoon of Dijon mustard, sometimes a teaspoon of honey, and freshly ground black pepper and salt. I then add fresh herbs according to the type of salad.

Dressings should be experimented with until you come up with the right taste for you. You only have to look on the shelves of any supermarket to see how vast the choice is in oils, vinegars and balsamic vinegar – so be guided by your taste buds. There's only one rule, don't drench your salad, otherwise it will just be a soggy mess. Be a little on the mean side – the leaves or vegetables should just glisten with the lightest coating. So toss gently and taste.

Butters for Hot French Bread

HERB BUTTER
Mash a few tablespoons of chopped fresh herbs —
parsley, chives and chervil, for example — into softened
butter. Shape into a roll, wrap in foil and chill until
needed.

ANCHOVY BUTTER
Blend about 1 (50 g/1¾ oz) can anchovies (or more or
less to taste) for each 225 g/8 oz butter, then mix in
the butter and shape as above.

Herbs

To accentuate, to enhance, add to, alter or adjust a
flavour, we use herbs. Even if you only have a kitchen
window sill, they are still well worth trying to grow.
You can buy small pots from nurseries, so it's easy to
have an instant herb garden. I've always found basil
the most temperamental — I don't know why, but most
are quite uncomplicated. If you have a garden, make
a herb patch — you won't regret it. Instead of paying
a ludicrous price for those tiny packets of fresh herbs
in the supermarket, you can just pick your own.

When cooking, be adventurous with herbs. Whatever a cookbook says — experiment.

Here is a reminder of the better-known herbs that
are easy to find in the shops: Rosemary, Mint, Dill,
Lemon Balm, Basil, Tarragon, Thyme, Bayleaf, Savory,
Parsley, Oregano, Sage, Marjoram, Chervil, Lemon
Grass, Fennel, Coriander and Cumin.

Home-made Tomato Sauce

Makes
900 ml/
1½ pints

25 g/1 oz butter
1 large onion, finely chopped
2 carrots, finely chopped
1 stick celery, finely chopped
1 (397 g/14 oz) can tomatoes
300 ml/½ pint tomato juice
2 tablespoons tomato purée
2 teaspoons sugar
2 teaspoons balsamic vinegar
1½ teaspoons Worcestershire sauce
some chopped herbs (your choice)
pinch of nutmeg
pinch of allspice
¼ teaspoon salt
black pepper

Home-made tomato sauce can be kept in the refrigerator or frozen. This sauce is great on spaghetti or as a filling for an omelette or with a meat loaf, and is also perfect to use as the base for a pizza topping.

Melt the butter in a saucepan, add the onion, carrots and celery and sauté until the onions are soft but not brown. Drain the tomatoes and reserve the juice, chop the tomatoes and add them to the sautéed vegetables. Add the juice from the can with the 300 ml/½ pint tomato juice (if you want a thinner sauce). Bring to the boil, then turn down the heat so that the sauce simmers gently for 15 minutes or longer.

Stir in the sugar, vinegar, Worcestershire sauce, herbs, spices and seasoning. When the carrots and celery are tender, you can purée this if you like a smooth sauce. I leave mine a bit chunky.

Easy Tomato and Basil Sauce

Serves 4

Good with any poached or cold white fish

Try pouring over not pasta – it's so fresh tasting (and simple)!

6 tomatoes
a few spring onions
1 tablespoon basil leaves
salt and pepper

Put all the ingredients in a food processor or liquidiser and keep whizzing until the mixture is pale and thick. Chill lightly before serving.

Dinner Parties

I think the most important thing to remember when giving a dinner party is to enjoy it yourself. Don't plan something that is going to send you into intensive care. Far better to have scrambled eggs on toast, a glass of wine and a laugh with friends, than an evening where your mind is panicking about what is going on in the kitchen. Here are a few menus that I have found work well – adjust them to suit your own style.

Just one more thing: always pay attention to the way your table looks. We used to go to dinner at someone's house, and in all the years we went, the table never changed: candles placed either side of a minute, dull flower arrangement – so boring. I have listed a few ideas just to get your imagination going.

Dinner party table settings

- Place small containers of wild flowers in front of each place setting.

- Try an old jug filled with buttercups and surrounded by bright yellow candles.

- Collect flowered side-plates from junk shops – it doesn't matter that they are all different, the effect will be lovely.

- Buy pretty sheets in the sales to use as tablecloths, and if you are handy with a needle, buy the pillow-cases as well and make extra-large napkins.

- A giant-sized cabbage with loose, floppy leaves can look stunning if you gently spread the leaves out from the centre and fill with pink, full-blown roses.

- Candlelight is so romantic to eat by. Light your dining room with candles only.

- Place a wine glass filled with flowers and herbs in front of each guest. Try rosemary, mint or lemon balm with snapdragons, cornflowers.

- If you find an old, but pretty teapot in a junk shop that has lost its lid, buy it – it will make an unusual container for flowers and lavender.

- A circle of flower-filled wineglasses, surrounding tall, white candles will look stunning.

- Suit your table to your food. If it's a pasta and salad evening, a check tablecloth with a table centre of leaves and globe artichokes with a few bright flowers added.

- I use baskets for everything and a really beautifully shaped basket with an old pudding bowl concealed inside, filled with flowers, can't be beaten.

- If you have a garden, you can always have something to put on your table. Try stems of blackberries or redcurrants, and there are also lots of weed-type flowers that can look terrific.

- If flowers are difficult to come by or expensive, use single stemmed vases, each containing one rose, or freesia, or lily.

- Decorate a basket of fruit (which could be your dessert) with flowers.

- In summer, use an old sun hat turned upside down and put a bowl in the crown. Fill with flowers.

- Fill a bowl with lemons and tuck some white daisies in between.

- When eating outside, geraniums (especially the scented ones) left in their pots and lined up with candles look very pretty.

- Fill a shallow basket with pansies, or use lots of small vases filled with small flowers instead of one centrepiece.

- When in doubt, go for simplicity.

Menu 1
To serve 4

Souffléed Tomatoes
or
Cherry Tomato Salad
*
Poached Turbot Steaks
Minted New Potatoes
Fresh Garden Vegetables
*
Fresh Figs with Goat's Cheese
Poppy Seed Straws

Souffléed Tomatoes

4 beefsteak tomatoes
25 g / 1 oz butter
20 g / ¾ oz flour
150 ml / ¼ pint milk
75 g / 3 oz Parmesan cheese, grated (it's best to use freshly grated if possible)
some basil leaves, chopped
salt
pinch of cayenne
3 eggs, separated
a few dried breadcrumbs

Cut a slice off the top of each tomato, then scoop out the seeds and turn upside down to drain while you make the soufflé mixture.

Melt the butter in a saucepan, stir in the flour and cook for a minute, then gradually add the milk, stirring all the time. Bring to the boil and cook for a minute — the sauce should be very thick. Beat in the cheese and basil, adding seasoning and cayenne to taste. Remove from the heat, add the egg yolks, beat well and set aside to cool slightly.

Blot the insides of the tomatoes with absorbent kitchen paper. Put a few breadcrumbs inside each tomato shell and roll them round tipping out any excess. Whisk the egg whites until they stand in stiff peaks, then stir a spoonful into the sauce. Carefully fold in the rest of the egg whites, divide the mixture between the tomato shells and bake in a hot oven (230C, 450F, gas 8) for 10 to 15 minutes, or until risen and brown. Serve immediately.

Cherry Tomato Salad

675 g / 1½ lb cherry tomatoes

some basil

6 tablespoons olive oil

juice of 1 lemon

salt and pepper

1 small red onion, finely chopped

1 teaspoon sugar

1 teaspoon mustard powder

lettuce or watercress to serve

Peel the tomatoes by covering with boiling water – for a moment or two – if you have time.

Put the whole tomatoes in a bowl with the leaves from the basil. Put all the rest of the ingredients in a screw-topped jar and shake well. Pour this over the tomatoes and mix thoroughly. Chill before serving on lettuce or watercress.

Poached Turbot Steaks

4 turbot steaks

1 carrot, quartered

1 onion, quartered

bay leaf

bunch of parsley (tied securely)

salt and pepper

150 ml / ¼ pint dry white wine

300 ml / ½ pint water

GOOSEBERRY SAUCE

450 g / 1 lb gooseberries
150 ml / ¼ pint water
pared rind of 1 lemon, cut into fine strips
50 g / 2 oz sugar
2 tablespoons cider vinegar
2 tablespoons chopped fresh dill
2 spring onions, chopped

GARNISH

mayonnaise
coarsely grated lemon rind
dill sprigs

Rinse and dry the fish steaks. Put all the remaining ingredients for cooking the fish in a large frying pan (a fairly deep one which has a lid) or a large flameproof casserole. If you have a fish kettle, then use that. Bring to the boil, then reduce the heat so that the liquid simmers and put the fish steaks in the pan. Cover and simmer gently for 10 minutes. Remove the pan from the heat and leave the fish to cool completely in the cooking liquid.

Top and tail the gooseberries, then put them in a pan with the water and lemon rind. Add the sugar and cider vinegar, bring to the boil. Reduce the heat and simmer for 10 minutes. Remove from the heat and add the remaining ingredients, leave to cool.

Lift the turbot out of the court bouillon, then remove the skin. Arrange the steaks on a serving dish. Top each fish steak with a little mayonnaise and grated lemon rind. Garnish with dill. Serve the sauce separately.

Fresh Figs With Goat's Cheese

Buy several different types of goat's cheese (or other creamy cheeses) and some fresh figs. Arrange the cheeses and halved figs on a large dish or wooden board and serve them with Poppy Seed Straws.

Poppy Seed Straws

50 g/2 oz rice flour
175 g/6 oz plain flour
100 g/4 oz butter
75 g/3 oz Cheddar cheese, finely grated
1 tablespoon poppy seeds
1 egg yolk

Mix the flours in a bowl, then rub in the butter and stir in the cheese and poppy seeds. Add the egg yolk to bind the mixture into a firm dough. Roll out on a lightly floured surface into a thin rectangle about 15 cm/6 in wide. Cut into strips (about 1 cm/½ in wide).

Grease one or several baking trays. Twist the strips of biscuit dough and place them on the trays, then bake in a moderately hot oven (200C, 400F, gas 6) for 12 to 15 minutes. Cool on wire racks.

Menu 2

To serve 4

Fresh Raspberry Soup
*
Ratatouille Quiche
Minted Wheat Salad
Green Salad
*
Grand Marnier Sorbet in
Chocolate Cups

Fresh Raspberry Soup

1 kg/2 lb raspberries
2 tablespoons icing sugar
150 ml/¼ pint Sauternes
300 ml/½ pint single cream

Purée the raspberries in a liquidiser or food processor, then press them through a sieve to remove the seeds. Sweeten the fruit purée with the icing sugar and stir in the wine with about two-thirds of the cream. Chill the soup really well before serving it. It should be *very* cold. Swirl the remaining cream on top.

If you don't want to use cream, use a large tub of plain yogurt instead.

Ratatouille Quiche

225 g/8 oz plain flour
salt and pepper
100 g/4 oz butter or sunflower margarine
50 g/2 oz Parmesan cheese, grated
about 3 tablespoons water
1 large aubergine
1 red pepper and 1 yellow pepper
1 green pepper
3 tablespoons olive oil

2 onions, sliced
2 cloves garlic, crushed
350 g/12 oz courgettes, sliced
1 (400 g/14 oz) can chopped tomatoes
2 bay leaves
few leaves of basil, chopped
1 teaspoon oregano
225 g/8 oz mozzarella cheese, sliced

Put the flour in a bowl and add a generous pinch of salt, rub in the butter or margarine until the mixture resembles fine breadcrumbs. Stir in the Parmesan and only just enough of the water to make the pastry bind together. Alternatively, if you have a food processor mix all the ingredients together in that adding water a teaspoonful at a time.

Roll out the pastry on a lightly floured board and use to line a 30 × 20 cm/12 × 8 in loose-bottomed quiche tin. Prick the base all over with a fork and line with a sheet of greaseproof paper. Sprinkle in some dried peas or beans and bake the pastry case in a moderately hot oven (200c, 400f, gas 6) for 15 minutes. Remove the paper and beans, then return to the oven for a further 10 minutes.

To make the filling, cut the stalk end and base from the aubergine, then chop the flesh. Place in a colander and sprinkle with salt. Leave on a draining board for 30 minutes. Cut the stalk ends off the peppers, remove any seeds and pith, then slice.

Heat the oil in a heavy-based frying pan – add sliced onions and garlic, and cook until soft but not browned. Remove, set aside. Dry the aubergine with absorbent kitchen paper, cook in oil for a few minutes then remove on to kitchen paper. Now repeat this process with the peppers. Remove. Wipe out pan. Return all the vegetables, plus courgettes and drained, canned tomatoes and herbs. Stir, add a little of the tomato juice. Simmer for 20 minutes covered, then uncover for 10 minutes. Check seasoning; the vegetables should be tender not mushy.

Spoon the filling into the pastry base and cover with the slices of mozzarella. Place the quiche on a

Aubergines love oil and will soak it up greedily – so try and be sparing with it.

flameproof plate and cook under a preheated grill until brown and bubbly. This can also be served cold.

Minted Wheat Salad

225 g/8 oz bulgur
bunch of spring onions
handful of raisins
50 g/2 oz pumpkin seeds, roasted
few sprigs of mint, chopped
grated rind and juice of 1 small lemon
1 clove garlic, crushed
6 tablespoons olive oil or sunflower oil
salt and pepper
lettuce hearts to serve (optional)

Soak the bulgur in cold water for about 30 minutes, then drain it thoroughly and put the grains in a bowl. Chop the spring onions and add them to the bulgur with the raisins, pumpkin seeds and mint.

In a screw-topped jar mix the lemon rind and juice, garlic, oil and plenty of seasoning. Shake well, then pour this dressing over the salad and toss. Marinate for at least 30 minutes. Arrange on lettuce leaves.

Grand Marnier Sorbet in Chocolate Cups

225 g/8 oz plain chocolate
SORBET
225 g/8 oz sugar
900 ml/1½ pints water
grated rind and juice of 2 oranges
6 tablespoons Grand Marnier
1 egg white

Melt the chocolate in a bowl over a saucepan of gently simmering water. Have ready eight paper cake cases, doubled up to make four extra thick ones. Coat the insides of these completely in chocolate, building up the coating as the chocolate sets. Leave in a cool place until the chocolate is hard.

You may need more chocolate for the cups so be prepared. Practise making them before you have a dinner party.

Dissolve the sugar in the water over low heat, then add the orange rind and juice and leave to cool. Stir in the Grand Marnier. Pour the syrup into a container and freeze until ice crystals are forming. Put the mixture into the food processor and whizz it round until the ice is broken down. Whisk the egg white until stiff, fold into the sorbet. Put back in the freezer until it is half frozen, then repeat the process twice to give a smooth sorbet without any ice crystals. If you have an ice cream making machine, freeze the sorbet in that. Once it is smooth, leave in the freezer for several hours or until hard.

To serve, remove the paper cases from around the chocolate cups and place them on individual plates. Leave the sorbet in the refrigerator for about 15 to 20 minutes before serving, so that it is soft enough to scoop. Use a small melon ball scoop and put a few sorbet balls into each chocolate cup.

Menu 3
To serve 4

Gazpacho
with
Anchovy Bread
*

Hot Lemon Chicken
with
Cold Herb Dressing
New Potatoes cooked
in their skins
*

Pink Grapefruit Tart

Gazpacho

| 1 thick slice wholemeal bread |
| 900 ml / 1½ pints tomato juice |
| 1 green pepper |
| 1 red pepper |
| 1 cucumber, peeled and chopped |
| bunch of spring onions, chopped |
| 450 g / 1 lb tomatoes, peeled and chopped |
| 2 cloves garlic, crushed |
| salt and pepper |
| juice of ½ lemon |
| dash of Worcestershire sauce |
| some fresh basil, chopped |

Cut the crusts off the bread, then break the slice up
and put it into the food processor or liquidiser with
half the tomato juice. Blend until smooth, put into a
large bowl.

Cut the tops off the peppers and remove the pith
and seeds from inside, chop the rest. Peel and chop
the tomatoes.

Put about a quarter of all the prepared vegetables in the liquidiser or food processor with the rest of the tomato juice, the garlic, seasoning and lemon juice. Blend until smooth and add to the first batch of tomato juice in the bowl. Add the Worcestershire sauce and basil and chill thoroughly.

Arrange the remaining finely chopped vegetables in a dish to serve with the soup.

Note: You can add some croûtons to serve with the soup if you like.

Anchovy Bread

1 short wholemeal French loaf
75 g/3 oz butter
anchovy paste to taste
2 tablespoons chopped parsley
a few drops of lemon juice

Cut the loaf almost through into slices, leaving them attached at the base. Beat the butter until soft, then beat in the anchovy paste, parsley and lemon juice. Spread this between the slices, wrap the loaf in foil and bake in a moderately hot oven (200c, 400f, gas 6) for 10 to 15 minutes. Separate the slices, put them in a napkin-lined basket and serve hot.

Hot Lemon Chicken with Cold Herb Dressing

1 large fresh roasting chicken (about 1.75 kg/4 lb in weight)
2–3 lemons
50 g/2 oz butter
DRESSING
a couple of handfuls of fresh herbs (the choice is yours) – chives, parsley, basil, mint (I use everything that's in the garden.)
50 ml/2 fl oz cider vinegar
1 tablespoon Dijon mustard
25 g/1 oz soft brown sugar
salt and pepper
juice of 1 lemon
250 ml/8 fl oz sunflower oil

Put the lemons inside the chicken. Put in a roasting tin and dot with the butter. Roast first on one side, then on the other in a moderately hot oven (190C, 375F, gas 5) for about 1½ hours, or until the chicken is cooked and the juices from the thickest part of the thigh run clear.

For the dressing, put the herbs in a food processor to chop, then add all the remaining ingredients; whizz them up to make a thick dressing.

Cut the chicken into serving pieces, arrange on a warm dish and pour over the cold dressing. Serve as soon as possible. The hot chicken and the cold dressing are an unusual combination.

Pink Grapefruit Tart

225 g/8 oz plain flour
175 g/6 oz butter
2 tablespoons caster sugar
1 egg yolk
FILLING
15 g/½ oz gelatine
3 tablespoons water
3 tablespoons caster sugar
300 ml/½ pint rosé wine
10–12 pink grapefruit (depending on size)
3 tablespoons redcurrant jelly, warmed

I know this sounds a lot of grapefruit but you really need this many.

Sift the flour into a bowl and rub in the butter, then add the sugar and egg yolk and mix the ingredients together to form a soft dough (or do this in a food processor). Wrap the dough in cling film and chill for at least 15 minutes. Have ready a 25 cm/10 in loose-bottomed tart tin or dish. Roll out the pastry thinly and line the tin. Prick the base all over and place a piece of greaseproof paper in the flan case. Sprinkle in some dried peas or beans to weigh the paper down, then bake in a moderately hot oven (200C, 400F, gas 6) for 20 minutes. Remove the paper and peas or beans, put back in the oven for a further 5 to 10 minutes, or until it is cooked and lightly browned. Leave to cool.

Soften the gelatine in the water then dissolve over gentle heat. Add the sugar to the rosé and stir until it dissolves. Stir in the gelatine and set aside. Cut all the peel and pith off the grapefruit. Use a sharp knife to cut between the membranes and remove the segments. Add any juice to the gelatine mixture and chill until it is half set.

Brush the bottom of the flan with a layer of redcurrant jelly. Arrange the fruit in the pastry case. Spoon the rosé glaze over the grapefruit and chill until it sets completely. Serve the tart fairly soon after it is made – this cannot be made hours and hours in advance or the juice from the fruit will soften the pastry.

Menu 4
To serve 4

Crudités with Dips
*
Glazed Ham with Oranges
Damson Sauce
Lightly steamed Mange-tout
New Potatoes
*
Emma's Almond and Pear Flan

Crudités with Dips

APPLE MINT DIP
225 g/8 oz cream cheese
a few spring onions, chopped
2 dessert apples, peeled, cored and grated
4 tablespoons natural yogurt
a few sprigs of mint, chopped

PEANUT AND AVOCADO DIP
50 g/2 oz salted peanuts
½ small onion, chopped
2 ripe avocado pears, peeled, stoned and cubed
1 clove garlic, crushed
150 ml/¼ pint soured cream
chilli powder to taste

CRUDITÉS
as many raw vegetables as possible
nasturtium leaves and flowers to garnish

Mix all the ingredients for the apple and mint dip and chill thoroughly. Put the peanuts and onion in a liquidiser or food processor and chop finely, then add all the remaining ingredients and process until smooth. Chill the second dip, not for too long or the avocado will discolour.

Prepare all the vegetables for the crudités. Arrange them on a large dish surrounding the bowls of dip. Add flowers to make it look decorative as well as edible.

Glazed Ham with Oranges

This is a simple traditional recipe but it is ideal for easy entertaining. The whole ham always looks nice and has the best flavour. It will, of course, serve about 30 people or leave you with plenty left over for other meals.

1 small whole gammon
250 ml/8 fl oz apple juice
6 tablespoons clear honey
generous pinch of ground cloves
1 teaspoon ground cinnamon
SPICED ORANGES
allow 1 orange per person
225 g/8 oz sugar
150 ml/¼ pint water
1 cinnamon stick
6 cloves
DAMSON SAUCE
450 g/1 lb damsons
2 tablespoons water
100 g/4 oz caster sugar
4 tablespoons port
GARNISH
rosemary
lemon balm

Soak the gammon for several hours (changing the water quite often). Calculate the cooking time at 25 minutes per 450 g/1 lb. If you have a large pan boil the gammon for 2 hours then roast it for the remaining time. Alternatively, roast the ham for the total cooking time. Put it in a roasting tin. Add the apple juice. Cover closely with foil and bake in a moderate oven (180c, 350f, gas 4) for the calculated time, or until the meat is cooked through. Carefully remove the skin and cut diamond shapes in the fat.

Mix the honey with the ground cloves, cinnamon, and the grated rind from two of the oranges. Brush this glaze over the gammon and put it back in the oven, uncovered, for a further 40 minutes, or until it is browned. Baste the ham several times with the honey and juices until cooked. Leave to cool completely (of course it can also be served hot).

To spice the oranges, cut off all the peel and pith and leave the fruit whole. Dissolve the sugar in the water with the cinnamon stick and the cloves added. When the sugar has dissolved, bring to the boil and cook until the syrup is just beginning to turn golden. Remove from the heat, pour over the oranges and leave to cool completely.

Halve and stone the damsons, then put them in a saucepan with the water and sugar. Heat slowly until the sugar melts, then continue to cook, stirring occasionally, for a few minutes. The damsons should be soft but not broken. Stir in the port and allow to cool before serving.

Place the ham on an extra large serving dish; arrange the oranges round it. Garnish with rosemary and lemon balm if it is going to be the centrepiece of a buffet.

Note: The ham tastes delicious if it is first boiled in apple juice. If serving the ham cold, make a large green salad with a herb dressing.

Emma's Almond and Pear Flan

BASE	
225 g/8 oz wholemeal digestive biscuits, crushed	
75 g/3 oz melted butter	
FILLING	
100 g/4 oz butter	
100 g/4 oz caster sugar	
3 eggs	
100 g/4 oz self-raising flour	
100 g/4 oz ground almonds	
1½ tablespoons milk	
½ teaspoon vanilla essence	
2 large ripe Comice pears, peeled, cored and quartered	
25 g/1 oz toasted almond flakes (optional)	

[handwritten note: This is my daughter Emma's recipe — and it's great hot or cold. You can use tinned pears — it still tastes wonderful.]

Make the base by mixing digestive biscuits with melted butter. Press into a 30 cm/12 in ovenproof flan dish.

Chill in the refrigerator.

To make the filling, beat the butter and sugar until the mixture looks pale. Beat in the eggs one at a time, then fold in the flour with the ground almonds, milk and vanilla essence.

Plunge the pears into boiling water and leave for 30 seconds then remove.

Spoon the creamed mixture into the flan case. (Don't worry if there doesn't seem to be enough because it rises.) Arrange the pears on top in an attractive pattern, pressing them lightly into the mixture. Bake in a moderately hot oven (200c, 400f, gas 6) for 20 to 25 minutes.

Serve warm sprinkled with toasted almond flakes.

Menu 5
To serve 4

Pistachio Pasta

*

Sole with Ginger Sauce
Fresh Spinach Salad

*

Redcurrant and Blackcurrant
Pudding

Pistachio Pasta

350 g / 12 oz pasta (whichever shapes you prefer)
bunch of spring onions
100 g / 4 oz pistachio nuts, chopped
2 bunches watercress
DRESSING
3 tablespoons olive oil (or sunflower oil if you prefer)
1 clove garlic, crushed
large handful of basil, chopped
2 tablespoons mild wholegrain or Dijon mustard (or use your favourite mustard)
3 tablespoons lemon juice
salt and pepper
150 ml / ¼ pint natural yogurt

Cook the pasta in plenty of boiling salted water for about 8 minutes, until it is just tender but not too soft. Drain and rinse immediately under cold water, then leave to drain thoroughly.

Chop the spring onions and mix them with the pistachio nuts in a large bowl. Set aside about half a bunch of watercress, then pick off the sprigs of the rest and put them in the bowl. Add the cooled pasta and toss well.

Put all the remaining ingredients (apart from the yogurt) in a food processor with the reserved watercress, with all the stalks and blend until smooth. Add the yogurt and pour this dressing over the salad.

Sole with Ginger Sauce

4 large sole fillets or 8 small ones
450 ml/¾ pint water
bay leaf
juice of ½ lemon
thinly pared rind of 1 lemon, cut into fine strips
40 g/1½ oz fresh root ginger, peeled and cut into very fine strips
1 teaspoon green peppercorns
salt and pepper
1 or 2 carrots, cut into very fine strips
2 egg yolks
4 tablespoons double cream or crème fraîche

Lay the sole fillets in a large deep frying pan, fish kettle or flameproof casserole. Pour in the water, add the bay leaf, lemon juice, pared rind and ginger. Sprinkle the peppercorns into the pan and add a little seasoning. Bring slowly just to the boil, then reduce the heat and poach the fish very gently for about 5 minutes, or until it is cooked. Carefully lift the fish out of the cooking liquid, lay the fillets on warm plates and keep hot, covered.

Bring the cooking liquid quickly to the boil and boil rapidly to reduce it to half its original quantity. Remove the bay leaf and add the carrot strips, then cook for 1–2 minutes to soften them slightly. Stir the egg yolks into the cream, then add a little of the hot fish liquid. Stir well and reduce the heat under the pan, pour the cream mixture into the sauce, stirring all the time. Heat through (but do not let the sauce boil). Pour a little of the sauce over the fish and serve the rest separately.

Fresh Spinach Salad

about a dozen or so young spinach leaves
1 lamb's lettuce
bunch of fresh young dandelion leaves
some marigold petals
DRESSING
several spring onions
a few sprigs of tarragon
3 tablespoons tarragon vinegar
about 150 ml/¼ pint sunflower oil
salt and pepper
generous pinch of sugar
generous pinch of mustard powder

Tear the spinach, lettuce and dandelion leaves into pieces and combine them in a bowl with the marigold petals and toss well. Put all the ingredients for the dressing in a screw-topped jar and shake until the mixture is smooth and well combined. Pour the dressing over the salad and toss just before you eat it.

Red- and Black-Currant Pudding

675 g/1½ lb blackcurrants
175 g/6 oz caster sugar
600 ml/1 pint plus 4 tablespoons water
50 g/2 oz gelatine
675 g/1½ lb redcurrants
about 20 sponge fingers
DECORATION
currant leaves
flowers

To remove currants from their stems run a fork down them – it makes this boring job much easier.

String the blackcurrants, then put them in a saucepan with half the sugar and just under 300 ml/½ pint water. Poach gently until the fruit is tender. Soften half the gelatine in 2 tablespoons water, then stir into the hot fruit until completely dissolved. Prepare the redcurrants in exactly the same way.

Dip the sponge fingers briefly in some of the fruit juices, then use them to line an 18 cm/7 in round tin, or charlotte mould, or a large pudding basin. When the fruit is half set, put layers of both types of fruit into the basin and chill thoroughly until set.

To serve, turn the pudding out and surround with sprigs of currants and their leaves. Cut the pudding into slices — the layers look quite spectacular.

Just Desserts

It goes without saying that fresh fruit salad is a delicious way to end a meal — or perhaps a bowl of blackberries, or strawberries with just a squeeze of orange juice, or raspberries out of the garden. Or a plate of fat, black cherries sitting on ice, or a solitary, perfect peach . . . the list is endless, but you don't need a recipe book for these. I am talking about wicked, calorie-ridden temptations. The following are for those guests who don't make desserts at home, but love to be offered them when they go out to dinner. We are all so conscious of cholesterol and calories that once in a while it's nice to break the rules. After all, tomorrow is another day . . . !

P.S. Dieters don't despair — I have included a few less fattening goodies in this section.

A Different Bread and Butter Pudding

Serves 10
to 12

50 g/2 oz butter
10 slices from a large loaf of white bread
225 g/8 oz sultanas
2 bananas, sliced
6 eggs
75 g/3 oz sugar
6 tablespoons rum or brandy
1.15 litres/2 pints milk

Fattening – but irresistible on a cold winter's day

Grease a large, not too deep, ovenproof dish. Butter the slices of bread and layer them with the sultanas and bananas. Beat the eggs, sugar, rum and milk together and pour over the bread, then chill for 1 hour so that the mixture becomes really moist.

Bake in a moderate oven (180C, 350F, gas 4) for 45 to 60 minutes.

Incredible Rice Pudding

Serves 6

100 g/4 oz sultanas
2 tablespoons rum
50 g/2 oz round-grain rice
450 ml/¾ pint milk
25 g/1 oz butter
1 tablespoon double cream
2 eggs, separated
50 g/2 oz sugar
pinch each of salt and nutmeg
300 ml/1 pint double cream, whipped (optional)

Always use fresh grated nutmeg.

Leave the sultanas to soak in the rum for as long as you wish.

Cook the rice in the milk until just tender, then stir in the butter and cream. Lightly beat the egg yolks and slowly stir in the rice, followed by the sugar, sultanas and rum, salt and nutmeg. Cook for a few more minutes. Cool.

Whisk the egg whites until stiff, fold into the rice mixture and pour into an ovenproof dish. Stand this in a roasting tin half filled with hot water and bake in a moderate oven (160C, 325F, gas 3) for 30 minutes, or until firm to the touch. This rice pudding is great whether served hot or cold. For those who don't count calories, allow the pudding to cool, then fold in the whipped cream and serve in wine glasses – it is worth starving next day for this!

Cloutie Dumpling
Serves 8

This is a traditional Scottish celebration pudding, although it is frequently served cold, sliced like a cake. The name is derived from the fact that the pudding is cooked in a cloth or 'cloutie'. Serve as a Christmas pudding with cream, custard or brandy butter.

350 g/12 oz plain flour
100 g/4 oz fresh white breadcrumbs
225 g/8 oz shredded suet
225 g/8 oz dark soft brown sugar
1 teaspooon baking powder
1 teaspoon mixed spice
1 teaspoon ground ginger
½ teaspoon cinnamon
1 tablespoon golden syrup
1 tablespoon marmalade
3 tablespoons black treacle
1 tablespoon milk
2 large carrots, grated
575 g/1¼ lb dried mixed fruit
2 large eggs, beaten

Mix all the ingredients together to make a fairly firm mixture. Put a clean pudding cloth, or large clean tea-towel, into a pan of boiling water and boil for 1 minute. Drain and when cool enough to handle, squeeze dry. Spread on a work surface and liberally sprinkle with flour: this forms the important seal or crust around the pudding during boiling. Spoon the mixture into the middle of the cloth and shape it into a neat round. Gather up the cloth and tie securely leaving room for the pudding to swell slightly. Bring a large saucepan of water to the boil. Put the dumpling into the pan, standing it on a trivet or an upturned saucer, cover and boil for 3 hours, topping up the water when necessary.

Remove from the pan, and leave the dumpling to stand for 5 minutes before removing the cloth. Serve hot, cut into slices.

Rich Carrot Dessert
Serves 8

6 eggs, separated	
175 g/6 oz soft brown sugar	
325 g/12 oz puréed cooked carrots	
1 tablespoon grated orange rind	
1 tablespoon grated lemon rind	
1 tablespoon brandy	
350 g/12 oz ground almonds	
50 g/2 oz self-raising flour	
1 carrot, grated	
1 teaspoon fresh or frozen orange juice	

Beat the egg yolks with the brown sugar until pale and thick. Add the puréed carrots, grated rinds, brandy, almonds, flour, grated carrot and fruit juice and gently fold the ingredients together until thoroughly mixed.

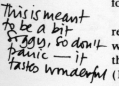
This is meant to be a bit soggy, so don't panic — it tastes wonderful

Beat the egg whites until stiff and fold them into the rest of the ingredients. Line a deep 22 cm/8½ in cake tin with greaseproof paper and grease it thoroughly. Pour the mixture into the tin and bake in a moderate oven (160C, 325F, gas 3) for 50 minutes or until a skewer comes out clean from the centre of the cake. Cool slightly in the tin, before turning out on to a wire rack. *Note*: This can also be served as an unusual cake to have at teatime.

Eli's Cheesecake
Serves 12

75 g/3 oz butter	
275 g/10 oz sugar	
250 g/8½22 oz chocolate digestive biscuits, crushed	
1/4 teaspoon nutmeg	
175 g/6 oz walnuts, ground	

| 4 eggs |
| 675 g/1½lb cream cheese |
| 100 ml/4 fl oz soured cream |
| 1 teaspoon vanilla essence |
| pinch of salt |
| 350 g/12 oz chocolate chips |
| DECORATION |
| curls of chocolate |
| icing sugar |

There is a restaurant in Chicago that is famous for its cheesecake and they gave me this recipe.

Melt the butter and 50 g/2 oz of the sugar together, mix in the crushed biscuits, nutmeg and ground walnuts, then press this mixture into the base of a 30 cm/12 in loose-bottomed cake tin and leave to set.

Whisk the eggs with the remaining sugar until pale and thick. Beat in the cream cheese until smooth, fold in the soured cream, vanilla essence, pinch of salt and chocolate chips and mix thoroughly. Pour the mixture over the biscuit base and bake in a moderate oven (180c, 350f, gas 4) for 1 hour, or until firm to touch.

Leave the cheesecake to cool before removing it from the tin, then refrigerate until required. Decorate with curls of chocolate and dust with icing sugar.

My Cheesecake
Serves 6 to 8

| 100 g/4 oz digestive biscuits, crushed |
| 75 g/3 oz, plus 1 tablespoon, caster sugar |
| 50 g/2 oz butter, melted |
| 1 teaspoon ground cinnamon |
| 450 g/1 lb Philadelphia cream cheese |
| 2 large eggs, beaten |
| few drops of vanilla essence |
| TOPPING |
| 300 ml/½ pint soured cream |
| 1 tablespoon caster sugar |
| few drops of vanilla essence |

If you want an extra creamy cheesecake, add a small carton of double cream to the Philadelphia cheese.

Mix the biscuits, 1 tablespoon caster sugar, melted butter and cinnamon. Press into the base of a greased 20 cm/8 in springform tin and chill while preparing the filling. Beat the cheese until smooth, then beat in the remaining ingredients. Pour over the base and place in a moderately hot oven (190c, 375f, gas 5). Bake for 25 minutes. Remove the cheesecake from the oven and increase the heat to very hot (240c, 475f, gas 9). Mix all the topping ingredients together and carefully spread the mixture over the top of the cheesecake. Replace in the oven for exactly 5 minutes. Remove, allow to cool, then chill overnight.

Good Old Tarte Tatin
Serves 6

225 g/8 oz plain flour	
100 g/4 oz butter, chilled and diced	
50 g/2 oz walnuts, ground	
100 g/4 oz sugar	
2 egg yolks	
FILLING	
75 g/3 oz butter	
175 g/6 oz sugar	
1–1.5 kg/2–3 lb Golden Delicious apples, peeled, cored and quartered	

For foolproof shortcrust pastry whirl 8oz plain flour, 3oz butter, 1oz lard and a pinch of salt in a food processor until it looks like breadcrumbs. Add one tablespoon of water. If it doesn't turn into dough add another. Stop processing as soon as the mixture turns into a ball. Knead briefly, wrap in greaseproof paper and chill for 15 minutes.

Sift the flour into a bowl, then rub in the butter until the mixture resembles fine breadcrumbs. Stir in the walnuts and sugar and work in the egg yolks to make a pastry dough. Wrap and chill the pastry while you prepare the filling.

For the tarte tatin you will need a shallow flame-proof dish or pan. Ideally a cast iron frying pan, with a handle short enough for the pan to fit in the oven; alternatively a flameproof gratin dish will do. Melt the butter and sugar together in the pan, then arrange the apple quarters, packed closely together, on top. The apples should fill the pan. Cook gently for about 20 minutes, or until the sugar forms a golden caramel. Remove from the heat and cool.

Roll out the pastry into a sheet large enough to cover the apples, with a little extra to tuck in round the sides. Lift the pastry over the apples and tuck the edges in neatly. Prick the dough all over with a fork, then bake in a moderately hot oven (190c, 375f, gas 5) for about 30 to 35 minutes or until the pastry is cooked. Cool until just warm in the pan, then place a serving plate over the top of the pan and invert the tarte tatin on to it. Serve warm.

Chocolate Roulade
Serves 6

175 g/6 oz plain chocolate
5 eggs, separated
150 g/5 oz caster sugar
75 g/3 oz plain flour
600 ml/1 pint double cream, whipped or crème fraîche
2 tablespoons rum
1 tablespoon icing sugar

Melt the chocolate in a bowl over hot water. In a mixing bowl, beat the egg yolks with the sugar until thick, light and creamy.

In another bowl, whisk the egg whites until stiff. Fold the flour, melted chocolate and egg whites into the sugar and yolk mixture. Pour the mixture into a lined and greased Swiss roll tin measuring 23 cm × 33 cm/9 × 13 in. Bake for 10 to 12 minutes in a moderately hot oven (190c, 375f, gas 5).

Remove the roulade from the oven, cover with a damp cloth and leave until cooled. Turn the cake out on to greaseproof paper which has been liberally sprinkled with icing sugar.

Whip 300 ml/½ pint of the cream with the rum and icing sugar and spread this evenly over the cake. Roll up the cake, then cover with the remainder of the cream, whipped until thick. Decorate by marking the cream along the length of the roulade with a fork.

Chill the cake until ready for serving, decorated with holly and sprinkled with icing sugar.

Prune and Apricot Pie
Serves 6 to 8

BASE
75 g/3 oz butter
50 g/2 oz sugar
225 g/8 oz digestive biscuits, crushed

FILLING

2 (225 g/8 oz) packets Philadelphia cream cheese
about 3 tablespoons icing sugar, sifted (or to taste)
2 tablespoons frozen concentrated orange juice
225 g/8 oz prunes, cooked and stoned
250 ml/8 fl oz double cream
225 g/8 oz dried apricots, cooked
flaked almonds, toasted, to decorate

To make the base, melt the butter over low heat then mix in the sugar and crushed biscuits. Press into the base and sides of a 20 cm/8 in loose-bottomed flan tin or pie plate and chill until firm.

For the filling, beat the cream cheese until smooth and soft, fold in the icing sugar, adding more to your taste if you like, and orange juice. Spread the mixture in the pie crust and refrigerate until set. Meanwhile, purée the prunes. Whip 150 ml/¼ pint of the cream until thick and fold in the prune purée. Purée the apricots too, whip the rest of the cream until thick and fold in the apricot purée.

Remove the crust from the tin or leave it in the pie plate and swirl the prune mixture around the outer edge of the pie, leaving a hole in the centre. Swirl the apricot mixture in the centre and decorate with toasted flaked almonds.

Pecan Pie
Serves 8

This is an authentic southern-style nut pie from the States.

PASTRY

225 g/8 oz plain flour
pinch each of salt and baking powder
1 teaspoon caster sugar
150 g/5 oz butter or block margarine, chilled
1 egg yolk
3–4 tablespoons milk

FILLING

3 large eggs	
175 g/6 oz golden syrup, warmed	
100 g/4 oz black treacle, warmed *or* soft brown sugar	
65 g/2½ oz butter, melted and cooled	
grated rind and juice of 1 lemon	
225 g/8 oz pecan halves	

To make the pastry, sift the flour, salt and baking powder into a bowl and add the sugar. Dice the butter or margarine, add to the flour mixture and rub in using your fingertips until the mixture resembles fine breadcrumbs. Mix the egg yolk with the milk and mix into the dry ingredients to make a soft, but not sticky, dough. Add a little extra milk if the mixture is too dry. Turn out on to a floured surface and knead lightly. Roll out and use to line a 25 cm/10 in flan tin. Chill.

For the filling, lightly beat the eggs until they are frothy, then stir in the golden syrup, black treacle or sugar, butter and lemon rind and juice. Mix well. Arrange the pecans in the base of the flan and pour over the egg mixture. Place the flan on a heated baking tray and bake in a moderate oven (180c, 350f, gas 4) for 1 hour or until set. Cool and serve with ice-cream.

Snowballs
Serves 6

6 large cooking apples	
6 tablespoons mincemeat	
1 tablespoon pine kernels	
265 g/9½ oz caster sugar	
1 tablespoon brandy	
4 egg whites	

Peel and core the apples. Mix the mincemeat with the pine kernels; mix 40 g/1½ oz of the sugar with the brandy. Stand the apples in a shallow baking dish, placing them well apart, and spoon the mincemeat mixture into the central holes left by the cores. Top with the brandy mixture, smoothing it over the top of the apples.

Whisk the egg whites until they are stiff, then gradually whisk in half the remaining sugar, then fold in the remainder. Pipe or spoon the meringue over the apples to completely cover them. Bake in a moderate oven (180C, 350F, gas 4) for 1 hour, or until the apples are just tender and the topping golden brown.

Melon and Lychees
Serves 4

Using a melon scoop, remove all the flesh from a ripe melon. Mix the melon with a (227 g/8 oz) can of lychees (drained) adding a dash of the juice from the can and chill for 30 minutes before serving. Arrange in individual glass dishes, or in the melon halves, and decorate with mint sprigs. If you like you can sprinkle the fruit with a little gin.

Chilled Orange Soufflé
Serves 6

2 tablespoons gelatine
300 ml/½ pint water
8 eggs, separated
2 (175 ml/6 fl oz) cans frozen concentrated orange juice
200 g/7 oz caster sugar
450 ml/¾ pint double cream
2 tablespoons orange liqueur
2 tablespoons chopped blanched almonds, lightly toasted

You can substitute frozen grapefruit juice if you prefer.

First prepare a 1.15 litre/2 pint soufflé dish. Tie a wide band of double thickness greaseproof paper around the outside of the dish. It should be high enough to stand at least 7.5 cm/3 in above the rim of the dish. Secure the band of paper with a piece of sticky tape and string. Sprinkle the gelatine over the water in a small bowl, set it aside for 5 minutes to soften, then dissolve it completely by stirring it over a saucepan of hot water. Set aside to cool. Beat the egg yolks until they are thick and pale, then whisk in the gelatine. Cook this mixture in its bowl over a saucepan of hot water, stirring continuously, until it has thickened enough to coat the back of a spoon. Take care not to boil the mixture, or to overcook it, or it will curdle. Remove from the heat and immediately stir in the orange juice. Chill for about 30 minutes, or until the mixture becomes syrupy in consistency.

Whisk the egg whites until they are foamy, then gradually pour in the sugar, whisking all the time, and continue to whisk until the mixture stands in stiff, glossy peaks. In a separate bowl, lightly whip 300 ml/½ pint of the cream with the orange liqueur. Fold the egg whites into the cream.

Carefully fold the cream mixture into the chilled orange custard, then pour the soufflé mixture into the prepared dish and chill thoroughly until set. To serve, carefully remove the paper collar: do this by easing it away from the mixture with the blade of a long knife. Whip the remaining cream until it stands in peaks. Press the nuts around the sides of the soufflé if you like, then pipe the cream around the top.

Chocolate Mousse
Serves 6

350 g/12 oz plain chocolate
150 g/5 oz butter
7 eggs, separated
4 tablespoons brandy, rum or Grand Marnier
CHOCOLATE LEAVES
100 g/4 oz plain chocolate
a few firm rose leaves

Very rich, so serve very little.

Melt the chocolate with the butter in the top of a double boiler or in a bowl over a saucepan of hot water. Beat in the egg yolks one at a time, then stir in the brandy, rum or Grand Marnier.

In a separate bowl, whisk the egg whites until they stand in stiff peaks, then fold them into the chocolate mixture. Pour or spoon the mousse into a glass serving dish or individual glass dishes and chill thoroughly; this mousse is best made the day before it is to be eaten, in which case the dishes should be covered with cling film when they are chilled.

To make the chocolate leaves for decoration, melt the chocolate in a double boiler or bowl over a saucepan of hot water. Spread or brush the chocolate over the leaves, on the side with the raised veins. Leave in a cool place until the chocolate has set, then carefully peel the leaves off and use the chocolate shapes to decorate the mousse.

Brown Bread Ice Cream
Serves 6

75 g/3 oz brown breadcrumbs
50 g/2 oz demerara sugar
4 eggs, separated
300 ml/½ pint double cream
50 g/2 oz caster sugar

Definitely not for dieters!

Mix the breadcrumbs and demerara sugar together, then grill them on the lowest setting until brown and crunchy (make sure they don't burn). Leave to cool.

Lightly beat the egg yolks. Whisk the double cream until thick. Finally whisk the egg whites to soft peaks and gradually whisk in the caster sugar until glossy. Fold all the ingredients together and freeze in a suitable container or an ice cream mould.

Frozen Chestnut Pudding
Serves 8

600 ml/1 pint double cream
175 g/6 oz caster sugar
6 eggs, separated
100 g/4 oz canned chestnuts, drained and chopped
1 tablespoon rum
DECORATION
300 ml/½ pint whipping cream, whipped
4 canned chestnuts, drained and sliced

Whip the double cream with a tablespoon of the sugar until thick; beat the egg yolks with 50 g/2 oz of the sugar until thick and light, then whisk the egg whites until stiff and gradually whisk in the remaining sugar. Gently mix the cream with the yolks and meringue mixture. Fold in the chestnuts and rum. Pack into a bombe mould or freezer-proof bowl and freeze until firm.

Dip the mould in hot water and turn out on to a plate. Decorate with cream and chestnut slices. Serve immediately.

Plum Ice Cream
Serves 6

This is a really easy ice cream recipe that doesn't need constant attention as it freezes, but still gives a smooth result.

1 kg/2 lb plums, stoned
175 g/6 oz sugar
300 ml/½ pint double cream
50 g/2 oz icing sugar
1 egg yolk
4 tablespoons Kirsch or brandy

Put the plums in a saucepan with any juice you have saved from stoning them. Add the sugar and cook gently, stirring occasionally, until the sugar melts. Poach the fruit for 5 minutes then purée it in a liquidiser or food processor. Leave to cool.

Whip the cream with the icing sugar, egg yolk and Kirsch or brandy until thick, then fold in the cooled fruit purée. Pour the ice cream mixture into a freezer container and freeze for several hours or overnight until firm. Leave the ice cream in the refrigerator for 5 to 15 minutes before scooping it out of the container.

Iced Bombe
Serves 8

Follow the recipe for Frozen Chestnut Pudding (page 114), omitting the chestnuts and rum. If you like, the ice cream can be left plain, or it can be flavoured with vanilla or mint essence, coffee or grated chocolate.

Pour the ice cream into a bombe mould or pudding basin and freeze until firm. When frozen, the middle of the bombe can be hollowed out and filled with grated chocolate, coffee liqueur beans, nuts or even a different flavoured ice cream. Pack some of the scooped-out ice cream on top of the filling and press down well. Re-cover and freeze again until needed. Decorate with whipped cream and preserved ginger.

Serve with a chocolate sauce, or a simple sauce made by melting a couple of Mars Bars in a basin over hot water.

Maraschino Cherry Ice Cream
Serves 12

900 ml / 1½ pints double cream
225 g / 8 oz caster sugar
8 eggs, separated
2 (230 g / 8.11 oz) jars maraschino cherries

Whisk the cream with 1 tablespoon of the sugar until very thick. Cover and chill. Whisk the egg whites until they form stiff peaks. Gradually whisk in 100 g / 4 oz of the remaining sugar until the meringue mixture is very thick and glossy, then fold in another 75 g / 3 oz sugar and set aside. Whisk the egg yolks with the last of the sugar until very thick and light. Stir the cream, meringue and yolk mixture together.

Drain and reserve the syrup from the cherries. Coarsely chop the cherries and fold them into the ice cream. Spoon into a freezer-proof container, cover and freeze overnight.

Serve scooped into an ice bowl (page 117) or delicate glasses. The maraschino juice can be served separately in a jug. If you wish, add a little liqueur to the maraschino juice.

Variation **Lychee Ice Cream** Purée 1 (312 g / 11 oz) can drained lychees in a liquidiser with a little of the syrup from the can. Fold the purée into the ice cream instead of the cherries.

Flower Ice Bowl

To make a flower ice bowl, you need some flowers or petals, a few sprigs of fern or a few delicate leaves; boiled, cooled water and two bowls. The bowls should be freezer-proof (china, tough glass or plastic) and one should hold twice the capacity of the other.

Half fill the larger bowl with cooled boiled water, then lower in the smaller one. Put stones or ice-cubes into the smaller bowl until the rims of both are level. Float the smaller one into the centre, with about 2.5 cm / 1 in of water between the bowls. Use tape to hold the bowls in position. Freeze for about 10 minutes.

Using a skewer or thin-bladed knife, poke flowers or petals, and bits of greenery in between the bowls. Replace the bowls in the freezer and leave for 24 hours. To use the ice bowl, remove the tape and the stones or ice cubes. Fill the small bowl with luke-warm water and gently twist it until it is free. Carefully lift the small bowl away from the ice. Dip the larger bowl in luke-warm water until the ice bowl can be loosened and lifted out. Replace the ice bowl in the freezer until ready to serve.

Used carefully, the bowl can be wiped out and reserved for other occasions. Smaller bowls can be made using soup or cereal bowls.

Everytime I make this I use diffent flowers or sometimes lemon or cucumber slices, or leaves. One of my favourites so far is Violets.

Grapefruit and Mint Sorbet
Serves 4 to 6

1 (410 g / 14½ oz) can grapefruit segments in natural juice
300 ml / ½ pint water
225 g / 8 oz sugar
2–3 sprigs of mint, finely chopped
2 egg whites

Put the grapefruit segments and juice, the water and sugar in a heavy-based saucepan. Heat gently until the sugar has dissolved. Bring to the boil and simmer for 5 minutes, then purée in a liquidiser. Cool.

Stir the mint into the cooled fruit purée and transfer it to a freezer-tray or container. Freeze until slushy. Stir well or whisk until smooth. Beat the egg whites to the soft-peak stage. Stir into the grapefruit mixture. Freeze until firm, stirring from time to time.

Quick Lychee Sorbet
Serves 4

1 (312 g/11 oz) can lychees
4 tablespoons icing sugar
juice of 1 large lemon

Put all the ingredients in a liquidiser or food processor and blend until smooth. Pour into a freezer container and freeze until half frozen, then return the mixture to the liquidiser or food processor and process until smooth. Pour the sorbet back into the container and freeze until hard. Leave in the refrigerator for about 20 minutes before serving.

Lavender Ice Cream
Serves 6

about 2–3 tablespoons lavender flowers
150 ml/¼ pint milk
pared rind of ½ lemon
4 tablespoons clear honey
300 ml/½ pint double cream

Make sure the lavender is clean and put it in a saucepan with the milk. Add the lemon rind, heat very slowly until the milk boils and leave to cool. Strain the milk, squeezing the lavender to extract all the flavour. Stir in the honey.

Whip the cream until just thick and slowly whisk in the milk. Pour into a freezer container and freeze until firm. Put in the refrigerator for about 20 minutes before serving.

Rose Petal and Pistachio Ice Cream

Serves
8 to 10

6 eggs
50 g/2 oz caster sugar
600 ml/1 pint milk
petals from two roses
300 ml/½ pint double cream
100 g/4 oz pistachio nuts, chopped

Separate 4 eggs, then put the yolks in a bowl with the remaining whole eggs and the sugar. Set the whites aside. Beat the eggs and sugar together until pale, then add the milk. Stand the bowl over a saucepan of barely simmering water and cook the mixture (stirring all the time) until it thickens enough to coat the back of a spoon. Do not overheat it or it will curdle. Remove the bowl from the heat and continue to stir until cooled.

Add the rose petals to the custard. Whip the cream until it forms soft peaks, then fold into the custard. Lightly stir in the nuts. Whisk the egg whites until they stand in stiff peaks, then fold them into the mixture and pour it into a freezer container or an ice cream maker. Freeze until icy, then whisk thoroughly and return the ice cream to the freezer. Repeat this process about three times, then leave the ice cream to freeze. If you are using an ice cream maker there is no need to whisk the ice crystals out of the mixture.

To serve, put the ice cream in the refrigerator for 20 to 30 minutes so that it is soft enough to scoop. Use rose petals to decorate individual portions of the ice cream.

Classic Summer Pudding

Serves 4 to 6

1.25 kg/2½ lb fruit, including redcurrants and blackcurrants, blackberries and raspberries
175 g/6 oz caster sugar
grated rind and juice of 1 orange
grated rind of 1 lemon
4 tablespoons port
1 small wholemeal loaf (or white if you prefer)
whole fruit to decorate

Put the currants and any other fruit which needs cooking in a saucepan with the sugar, fruit rinds and juice. Poach gently until the juice runs and the fruit is softened. (You can also use strawberries, rhubarb, cherries, peaches and plums in summer pudding.)

Mix all the types of fruit together and stir in the port. Cut the crusts off the bread and slice it fairly thinly. Line a 1.15 litre/2 pint pudding basin with the bread, then put the fruit in and top with more bread. Cover and weight down, chill for several hours. Reserve any remaining fruit juice to pour over the pudding when it is turned out or whip the juice into the double cream until thick.

Ease the blade of a palette knife between the pudding and the basin to loosen the pudding, then invert it on to a serving dish and pour over any reserved juice. Surround the pudding with lots of whole fruit — currants and soft fruit. Serve with whipped cream.

Apricot Tarts
Makes 12

SWEET PASTRY
100 g/4 oz plain flour
65 g/2½ oz butter
25 g/1 oz caster sugar
1 egg yolk

CRÈME PÂTISSIÈRE
25 g/1 oz cornflour
25 g/1 oz caster sugar
300 ml/½ pint milk
vanilla pod
2 egg yolks
2 tablespoons double cream

TOPPING
6 ripe apricots

GLAZE
3 tablespoons apricot jam

Sift the flour for the pastry into a bowl, then rub in the butter and stir in the sugar. Add the egg yolk and mix to make a smooth soft pastry. Chill briefly, then roll out thinly and use to line 12 small tart tins. Prick the pastry with a fork and chill the tart cases for 30 minutes before cooking them. Bake in a moderately hot oven (200c, 400f, gas 6) for about 15 minutes, or until the pastry is cooked and pale brown. Leave in the tins for a minute or so, then carefully lift the tart cases and transfer them to a wire rack to cool completely.

Blend the cornflour to a smooth paste with the sugar and a little of the milk. Pour the rest of the milk into a saucepan and add the vanilla pod, splitting it to release the flavour. Bring to the boil over a low heat, then leave to stand for 5 minutes before removing the pod. Pour the milk on to the cornflour mixture, stirring all the time, then return to the pan and bring back to the boil, again stirring to prevent the mixture from becoming lumpy. Remove from the heat and beat in first the egg yolks then the cream. Leave to cool.

Peel, halve and stone the apricots. Heat the jam in a small saucepan, sieve if you have time. When the crème pâtissière has cooled divide it between the tart cases and chill until set. Put an apricot half on each tartlet and brush the glaze over the top. Chill lightly before serving.

Note: If you can be bothered, crack open the apricot stones and sprinkle the kernels over the tarts, or top with toasted almonds. Use other fruits for this as they come into season.

Greengage Dessert
Serves 4 to 6

This is so simple – but it is a lovely way of using greengages.

450 g / 1 lb greengages
3 tablespoons honey
2 tablespoons water
300 ml / ½ pint double cream
a few hazelnuts, chopped and toasted

Stone the greengages and place in a saucepan with the honey and water. Cover and cook over a gentle heat until soft. Purée the fruit in a food processor. When

cold, whip the cream until thick and fold into the fruit
purée. Spoon into individual glasses and sprinkle with
the chopped nuts.

Note: I also use plums for this.

Blueberry-Filled Cheesecake
Serves 6 to 8

BASE
100 g/4 oz digestive biscuits, crushed
50 g/2 oz hazelnuts, toasted and chopped
50 g/2 oz butter
BLUEBERRY FILLING
450 g/1 lb blueberries plus some whole ones for decoration
25 g/1 oz caster sugar
15 g/½ oz gelatine
3 tablespoons water
CREAM CHEESE FILLING
225 g/8 oz cream cheese
grated rind and juice of 1 lemon
50 g/2 oz caster sugar
150 ml/¼ pint natural yogurt (use the very creamy thick Greek-type)
3 tablespoons orange liqueur
15 g/½ oz gelatine
3 tablespoons water
2 egg whites

Mix the crushed biscuits with the nuts. Melt the butter
and stir in the biscuit mixture. Press this into the base
of an 18 cm/7 in springform tin and chill.

First make the blueberry filling. Put the blueberries
in a pan with the sugar and cook gently for just a few
minutes until the juice runs then remove from the
heat. Dissolve the gelatine in the water over a pan
of simmering water, then stir it into the blueberries
and leave until almost set.

Beat the cream cheese with the lemon rind and
juice, then stir in the sugar and the yogurt. Add
the liqueur, stir and set aside. Soften the gelatine

in the water then dissolve over low heat. Stir it into the cream cheese mixture and chill until half set. Whisk the egg whites until stiff, then fold them into the mixture.

Put half the cream cheese on top of the biscuit crust, spreading it out evenly. Spoon the half-set blueberry mixture on top, then add the rest of the cream cheese mixture. Smooth the top and chill until completely set.

To remove the cheesecake from the tin, gently run a knife around the inside, then undo the springform sides. Top the cheesecake with whole blueberries, piled up in the middle just before you serve it.

If you don't care about calories, serve the cheese-cake with cream flavoured with orange liqueur.

Redcurrants with Yogurt
Serves 6

This looks nice served in wine glasses.

450 g / 1 lb redcurrants
600 ml / 1 pint Greek yogurt
honey to taste
redcurrants on stalks to decorate

String the redcurrants and chill them thoroughly. Make sure that the yogurt is really well chilled.

Stir the honey into the yogurt. Layer the redcurrants and yogurt into a glass dish, then decorate with currants on their stalks. The dessert should be served very cold.

Note: Equally delicious with blackberries or black-currants.

Redcurrants with Melon
Serves 4

450 g (1 lb) redcurrants, topped and tailed
3 tablespoons sugar
1 Charentais melon

Place the redcurrants and sugar in a small pan and cook, over a very low heat, until the sugar has dissolved and the juices run from the fruit. Whirl in a blender or food processor, strain through a sieve and chill.

Peel the melon, remove the seeds and cut lengthways into very thin slices. Arrange on a large plate in a fan shape.

Carefully spoon the chilled redcurrant sauce over the melon to serve.

Sweet Carrot Tart
Serves 6 to 8

225 g/8 oz plain flour
100 g/4 oz butter or margarine
about 3 tablespoons water
FILLING
100 g/4 oz carrots, grated
25 g/1 oz raisins
1 teaspoon grated nutmeg
2 eggs
150 ml/¼ pint double cream
75 g/3 oz wholemeal breadcrumbs
4 tablespoons brandy
grated rind and juice of 1 orange
a little lemon juice

Sift the flour into a bowl and rub in the butter, then stir in the water to bind the ingredients. Roll out the pastry and use to line a 20 cm/8 in loose-bottomed flan tin. Prick the base all over and place a piece of greaseproof paper in the flan tin. Sprinkle in some dried peas or beans to weigh the paper down, then bake in a moderate oven (180C, 350F, gas 4) for 10 minutes. Remove the paper and peas or beans.

Beat all the filling ingredients together, pour into the flan and continue to cook for a further 40 minutes, until lightly golden and firm to the touch. Serve warm or cold.

Tricia's Apple Crisp
Serves 8

6 Granny Smith apples, peeled, cored and very thinly sliced

juice of 3 lemons
175 g (6 oz) plain flour
2½ teaspoons ground cinnamon
pinch of salt
175 g (6 oz) butter
350 g (12 oz) soft brown sugar
50 g (2 oz) pecans, chopped
50 g (2 oz) walnuts, chopped

Layer the apples in a 20 cm/18 in greased round cake tin or 25 × 15 cm 8 × 6 in rectangular baking dish, sprinkling lemon juice between each layer.

Sift the flour with the cinnamon and salt. Rub in the butter until the mixture resembles fine breadcrumbs. Stir in the sugar and nuts. Spoon evenly over the apple mixture, pressing down firmly.

My daughter Sarah gave me this recipe — it's great!

Bake in a moderate oven, (180c/350F/gas 4), for 50–60 minutes, or until the apples are cooked and the topping is crisp and golden brown.

Serve hot with ice cream.

Green Gunpowder Tea Ice Cream
Serves 4 to 6

150 ml (¼ pint) freshly-made strong green gunpowder tea
juice of ½ lemon
4 egg yolks
100 g (4 oz) caster sugar
600 ml (1 pint) double cream

Mix the cold tea with the lemon juice. Beat the egg yolks with the sugar until thick and creamy. Heat the cream until very hot but do not allow to boil. Beat into the egg mixture, blending well. Add the tea and stir, over a very gentle heat, until the mixture begins to thicken and will coat the back of a spoon. Allow to cool then pour into a freezer tray. Freeze for about 1–2 hours, or until mushy.

Remove from the freezer and whisk to break down any large ice crystals. Return to the freezer tray and freeze until firm.

Remove the ice cream from the freezer about 20 minutes before required to soften slightly. Serve scooped into chilled wine glasses.

Fresh-tasting Raspberry Mousse for Dieters
Serves 4

100 g (4 oz) raspberries, hulled
15 g (½ oz) sugar
7 g (¼ oz) powdered gelatine
1 tablespoon boiling water
450 ml (¾ pint) thick natural yogurt
a few fresh raspberries or sliced strawberries to decorate

Purée the raspberries in a blender or food processor. Sieve to remove the pips then mix with the sugar. Dissolve the gelatine in the water and stir into the raspberry mixture.

Fold in the yogurt and pour into a serving dish. Cover and chill for not less than 3 hours. Serve decorated with a few fresh raspberries or sliced strawberries.

Fooled mango is the perfect light dessert to serve after a hearty main course. Purée the flesh of 2 very ripe mangoes with the juice of 1 lime and 1 heaped tablespoon of clear honey. Whip the cream until thick and fold into the mango purée. Serve chilled in tall wine glasses. SERVES 4.

Plums in Grand Marnier
Serves 4

75 g (3 oz) caster sugar
300 ml (½ pint) water
450 g (1 lb) red plums, left whole
grated rind of 1 orange
3 tablespoons Grand Marnier

Place the sugar and water in a heavy-based pan and heat gently until the sugar dissolves. Add the plums and orange rind and simmer gently for about 10–15 minutes, or until the plums are cooked.

Stir in the Grand Marnier and transfer to a serving bowl. Serve warm or cold with whipped cream.

Melon Jelly
Serves 4

1 honeydew melon
juice of 1 lemon
75 g / 3 oz caster sugar
25 g / 1 oz gelatine
4 tablespoons water
150 ml / ¼ pint apple juice
fresh mint sprigs, finely chopped

Halve the melon, remove the seeds, then scoop out the flesh and place it in a liquidiser or food processor with the lemon juice and caster sugar. Purée until smooth.

Soften the gelatine in the water then dissolve over gentle heat. Add this to the apple juice, then pour it into the purée and whisk in the mint.

Pour into a 1.4 litre / 2½ pint mould and chill until set.

Turn the jelly out and serve decorated with lots of mint sprigs.

Alternatively, the mixture can be frozen until slushy, then whisked until smooth and refrozen until firm to make a melon sorbet. If you do this, then omit the gelatine.

Note: You can also return the jelly to the melon skins, then, when set, cut into slices and serve.

Rhubarb Mousse in a Coconut Crust
Serves 6

450 g / 1 lb rhubarb
150 ml / ¼ pint plus 4 tablespoons water
50 g / 2 oz sugar
50 g / 2 oz butter
75 g / 3 oz flaked coconut
25 g / 1 oz gelatine
300 ml / ½ pint double cream

Trim and slice the rhubarb, then put it in a pan with the 150 ml / ¼ pint water and the sugar. Bring to the boil, then reduce the heat and cook gently for about 5 or 10 minutes or until the rhubarb is tender. Blend the fruit in a food processor or liquidiser.

Melt the butter in a saucepan and add the coconut, cook for a few minutes over a low heat to let it brown slightly. Press into a 23 cm/9 in shallow dish and leave to set in the refrigerator.

Soften the gelatine in the 4 tablespoons water then dissolve over low heat. Stir into the rhubarb and leave until half set. Lightly whip the cream and fold it into the fruit, then pile it into the coconut crust. Chill until firm.

Useful Pancakes

MAKES ABOUT 24 PANCAKES

225 g/8 oz plain flour (or you can use wholemeal flour or half-and-half wholemeal and buckwheat flours)
2 large eggs
generous pinch of salt
600 ml/1 pint milk
butter or oil, or a mixture of both, for cooking

Sift the flour into a bowl. Make a well in the middle and crack in the eggs. Add the salt and some of the milk, then beat well, gradually incorporating the flour and adding more milk to make a smooth batter. Continue beating for a few minutes, then leave the batter, covered, to stand for at least 30 minutes.

To cook pancakes, heat a heavy frying pan and grease it with a little butter or oil. Pour a spoonful of batter on to the pan and tilt it so that the mixture runs all over the surface. Cook until the pancake is golden underneath, then turn it over (or toss it if you are brave, or very competent, or both) and cook on the other side until golden. Continue cooking the pancakes in this way, layering them with pieces of absorbent kitchen paper or greaseproof paper to stop them from sticking together. Add a little water to the batter to keep it thin – if the batter is too thick the pancakes will be heavy. The pancakes can be served hot, but they are also good cold, with different fillings.

| Pancake Ideas: | Serve the pancakes hot or cold in any of the following ways. |

| With Rum Bananas: | Quickly fry some sliced bananas in butter, add demerara sugar and rum and stir over high heat for a minute. Serve hot pancakes with Greek yogurt and whipped cream. |

| With Mock Caviar: | Serve filled with mock caviar and soured cream with chives. |

| With Sliced Mango: | Fill with sliced mango, fold over and sprinkle with brown sugar. Put under the grill briefly. |

Gratin of Pancakes
Serves 4 to 6

The pancakes can be made ahead and frozen. You can replace the fruit with Luxurious Mincemeat. (page 236) Serve with ice cream.

PANCAKES

100 g/4 oz plain flour

1 egg

450 ml/¾ pint milk

1 teaspoon sugar

1 tablespoon melted butter

FILLING

225 g/8 oz Philadelphia cream cheese

75 g/3 oz caster sugar

grated rind and juice of 1 lemon

1 banana, thinly sliced

2 peaches, thinly sliced

3 slices fresh pineapple, chopped

2 oranges, peeled and cut into segments

3 tablespoons chopped almonds or hazelnuts, lightly toasted

TOPPING

4 egg yolks

100 g/4 oz caster sugar

3 tablespoons brandy, sherry or rum

To make the pancakes, sift the flour into a bowl. Gradually beat in the egg and milk until a smooth batter is formed. Stir in the sugar and butter and, if possible, leave the batter to stand for a couple of hours. Cook the pancakes in a heavy-based or non-stick frying pan, using a little melted butter or oil to prevent them from sticking to the pan. Stack the cooked pancakes on a plate with sheets of greaseproof paper between them to prevent them from sticking together. You will need ten pancakes for the gratin.

To make the filling, cream the cheese with the sugar, lemon rind and juice. Gently warm the pancakes in a frying pan with a little butter. Stack the pancakes, layering them alternately with the cream cheese mixture and the fruit. Top with the nuts.

To make the topping, whisk the egg yolks with the sugar and brandy until thick and frothy (this may be easier in a bowl over hot water, or in the top of a double boiler). Spoon this over the pancakes and place under a hot grill until golden brown and bubbling. Cut into wedges (like a cake) and serve.

Nut Clusters

Makes
about 24

450 g / 1 lb dark plain dessert chocolate
175 g / 6 oz mixed nuts, chopped (try almonds, hazelnuts and walnuts)
25 g / 1 oz crystallised ginger, chopped
50 g / 2 oz candied peel, chopped

Melt half the chocolate in a bowl over a pan of hot water. Stir in the nuts, ginger and peel. Line a baking tray with waxed or non-stick baking paper. Put heaped teaspoonfuls of the mixture on the paper and leave in a cool place to set overnight. Next day, melt the remaining chocolate in the same way and, using two forks, quickly dip the nut clusters into the chocolate to coat them evenly. Leave to set on the paper, as before.

Note: If you like you can simply mix the ingredients into all the melted chocolate and allow the spoonfuls of mixture to set.

Truffles
Makes about 60

350 g/12 oz digestive biscuits, crushed
100 g/4 oz walnuts, chopped
2 tablespoons golden syrup
100 ml/4 fl oz rum or brandy
7–8 tablespoons cocoa powder, sifted
100 g/4 oz caster sugar

Thoroughly mix the crushed biscuits, nuts, syrup, rum or brandy, 2 tablespoons of the cocoa powder and the caster sugar in a bowl. Shape the biscuit mixture into small, walnut-sized balls and roll each one in the remaining cocoa powder. Chill thoroughly before serving.

Dipped Fruits

Californian or New Zealand strawberries are now available at Christmas time. Melt plain dessert chocolate in a bowl over a pan of hot water, stir gently until smooth and dip the strawberries into the chocolate so that they are half coated. Lay them on a baking tray lined with non-stick baking paper and leave in a cool place until set. If strawberries are out of the question, try dipping cherries or mandarin segments.

Crystallised Fruits

It is important to choose firm ripe fruit. Suitable fruits are pineapple slices (peeled and cored), stoned and halved apricots or plums, whole small pears, peeled or whole mandarins. If you are going to cook small fruits whole, it is best to prick them well so the sugar syrup can be absorbed easily. Soft fruits such as berries are not suitable. The prepared fruit should be weighed and put into a large, heavy-based saucepan (not aluminium). Pour in 300 ml/½ pint of water to every 450 g/1 lb of fruit. Cover and simmer gently until the fruit softens – about 15 minutes for pineapple slices or 2 to 3 minutes for softer fruits. Carefully lift out the fruit and measure the liquid in the pan. Pour the liquid back into the pan and add 125 g/4½ oz powdered glucose and 50g/2 oz of granulated sugar to every 300 ml/½ pint of liquid. Stir over low heat until the sugar and glucose dissolves. Bring to the boil and simmer for one minute. Remove from the heat and add the fruit. Cover with a piece of damp greaseproof paper and leave overnight. Next day, remove the fruit from the pan. As before, measure the syrup and this time add 50 g/2 oz sugar to every 300 ml/½ pint of liquid. Put the liquid and the sugar into the pan, dissolve and simmer as before. Add the fruit, off the heat, cover the pan and leave overnight. Do this every day for the next five days, then increase the sugar to 75 g/3 oz and repeat as before, this time leaving the fruit undisturbed for 48 hours. Repeat this last process once more. When the final 48 hours is up, drain the fruit from any syrup that is left and put it on a cooling rack to dry. This can be done in an airing cupboard (set the rack over a baking tray to catch any drips) or in any other place that is warm and dry. When the fruit feels dry (not sticky) to touch it's ready. Store in airtight containers, lined with greaseproof or waxed paper and keep in a cool, dry place.

Boxing Day Alternative Pudding
Serves 8

6 oranges
4 pink grapefruit
2 ordinary grapefruit
4 tangerines
chopped mint

Most of these recipes are "proper puddings". Although they are great as an occasional treat, fruit is usually the nicest and simplest way to end a meal.

Slice all the skin and pith from the citrus fruits. Slice the flesh as thinly as possible. Arrange the prepared fruit in a large dish, overlapping the slices: start with the tangerines in the middle, then the white and pink grapefruit and the oranges. Pour over any orange juice that may have escaped in the slicing and sprinkle with chopped mint. Cover with cling film until needed.

This salad is ideal for Christmas dieters or for those who would like a change from rich food. Serve any leftover fruit for breakfast next day.

Celebrations

There are occasions when a celebration is called for, and if you decide to celebrate at home with friends – then a bit of planning won't come amiss . . .

Dinner for 20

Cream Cheese and Vegetable Loaf
*
Fruit-filled Chicken
Chicken stuffed with Pistachios
and Rice
Cool Parsley Sauce
Scrubbed Potato Salad
Nasturtium Salad
*
Whole Cheese with Fresh Figs and
Apricots
Home-made Oatcakes
Selection of Biscuits
*
Plum Pyramid
or
Apple and Mint Sorbet

A Time Guide

Up to a week before	Make the meringues for the plum pyramid. Keep in airtight containers.
	Make the sorbet and keep it in the freezer.
	Buy the cheese.
	Make the oatcakes and store them in an airtight container.

•

Two days before	Bone the chickens (or better still ask your butcher to do it). Prepare the stuffings, keep in the refrigerator.

•

The day before	Stuff and cook the chickens.
	Prepare, but do not dress, the salads.
	Make the dressings and keep in the refrigerator.
	Make the cream cheese loaf.

•

On the morning	Do the flowers and decorations, put out candles.
	Slice the chickens, cover and chill.
	Turn out the cream cheese loaf, cover and chill.
	Put out the cheese and prepare the fruit.

•

Two hours before	Lay the table.

•

One hour before	Dress the salads.
	Assemble the meringue pyramid.

•

When the first course is served	Transfer the sorbet to the refrigerator.

Cream Cheese and Vegetable Loaf

MAKE TWO OF THESE
675 g/1½ lb cream cheese
1 tablespoon chopped fresh basil
1 small onion, finely chopped
4 tablespoons mayonnaise
salt and pepper
225 g/8 oz asparagus, cooked until just tender
100 g/4 oz carrots, cut into fine strips and cooked
50 g/2 oz broken walnuts
100 g/4 oz French beans, cooked
large handful of parsley, chopped

Beat the cream cheese with the basil, onion, mayonnaise and seasoning to taste. The vegetables should be steamed so that they retain all their colour and texture.

Line a 1 kg/2 lb loaf tin with greaseproof paper and grease it with a little sunflower oil. Layer the cream cheese mixture with the vegetables, ending with a layer of cream cheese. Cover and chill for several hours, or overnight, until the mixture is firm.

Turn the loaf out and peel away the greaseproof paper, then cover it completely with chopped parsley, pressing the herb on with the blade of a knife. This is nice served with a tomato salad.

Fruit-Filled Chicken

If you have a good butcher, then ask him if he will bone the chickens for you.

1 fresh roasting chicken (about 1.75 kg/4 lb in weight)
STUFFING
350 g/12 oz prunes, soaked overnight and stoned
8 oranges
2 lemons
2 limes
100 g/4 oz wholemeal breadcrumbs
150 ml/¼ pint Madeira
salt and pepper

To bone the chicken, lay it breast side down and use a sharp knife to cut down the middle. Work on one side at a time and cut as close to the bones as possible removing all the meat. Take great care not to make any cuts in the skin and cut a fine sliver off the breastbone to prevent this. Once you have done one side, turn the chicken round and work down the second side.

Cut the prunes into pieces and put them in a bowl. Grate the rind from 2 oranges and add to the prunes, then remove all the peel and pith from the oranges. Use a small, sharp knife to cut between the membranes and remove the fruit segments. Add these to the prunes. Coarsely grate the rind from the lemons and limes and add to the stuffing with the breadcrumbs and Madeira. Mix well.

Put the stuffing in the chicken, fold the meat over and sew up the opening securely, to make a fairly long roll. Put this in a roasting tin and sprinkle with plenty of seasoning. Dot with the butter and roast in a moderately hot oven (190c, 375f, gas 5) for about 1¼ hours, or until the chicken is cooked and browned. Wrap the cooked chicken completely in foil and leave it to cool. To serve, slice as thinly as possible and arrange on a serving dish.

Chicken Stuffed with Pistachios and Rice

1 large roasting chicken (about 1.75 kg/4 lb in weight)
STUFFING
225 g/8 oz long-grain brown rice
100 g/4 oz pistachio nuts, chopped
bunch of spring onions
1 large onion, chopped
1 clove garlic, crushed
50 g/2 oz butter
bunch of watercress, finely chopped
salt and pepper
2 tablespoons double cream
a few sprigs of tarragon, chopped
small cup of parsley, chopped
2 tablespoons dry sherry

Bone the chicken or ask your butcher to do this for you.

Cook the brown rice in boiling salted water. Mix the nuts with the rice, add the spring onions. Cook the chopped onion with the garlic in the butter until soft, then add to the stuffing with the watercress, plenty of seasoning, the cream and the herbs. Stir in the sherry and use this stuffing to fill the chicken.

Roast in a moderately hot oven (190C, 375F, gas 5) for about 1¼ hours or until the chicken is cooked through and tender then wrap it in foil until cool.

Nasturtium Salad

10 lettuce hearts, halved
Nasturtium petals
bunch of spring onions, chopped
300 ml / ½ pint olive oil
2 cloves garlic, crushed
3 tablespoons mild mustard
50 ml / 2 fl oz wine vinegar
2 teaspoons sugar

Toss the lettuce and petals in a large bowl. Put all the other ingredients into a liquidiser or food processor, then whizz them up until smooth. Pour over the salad at the last minute.

Brie with Figs and Apricots

Buy one ripe brie from a good cheese shop. Make sure that it is in tip-top condition because it is not possible to ripen a poor cheese at home. Have fresh apricots and figs to serve with the cheese and offer a selection of plain biscuits, some of them home-made. Why not make the oatcakes?

Arrange on a basket, with leaves and flowers to decorate.

Oatcakes

MAKE TWO LOTS
100 g/4 oz plain flour
100 g/4 oz medium oatmeal
salt
75 g/3 oz butter
1 tablespoon caster sugar
1 egg

Put the flour, oatmeal and a generous pinch of salt in the food processor with the butter and sugar. Whizz the ingredients until the butter is blended in, then add the egg and mix until a dough is formed.

Turn this out on to a floured board and roll it out very thinly. Use a plain biscuit cutter to cut out the biscuits, then put them on a greased baking tray and bake in a moderate oven (180c, 350f, gas 4) for about 15 to 20 minutes or until the biscuits are golden brown. Leave the oatcakes on the trays for a few minutes, then transfer them to wire racks to cool completely.

Apple and Mint Sorbet

MAKE THREE LOTS
600 ml/1 pint apple juice
small bunch of mint (apple mint if you have it), chopped
100 g/4 oz sugar
2 egg whites

Pour the apple juice into a saucepan and add the mint. Stir in the sugar and heat gently, still stirring, until all the sugar has dissolved. Leave to cool, then pour the syrup into a freezer container or ice cream maker.

Freeze until half frozen, then remove and whisk thoroughly to break down all the ice crystals. Whisk the egg whites until they are stiff, fold them into the slushy mixture and put it back in the freezer. Whisk the water ice another three times during freezing, to break down the crystals and produce a smooth result.

When the mixture is smooth, leave it to freeze until hard. Put the water ice in the refrigerator for about 20 minutes before scooping it out of the container. Use an ice cream scoop and place in a flower ice-bowl or on to a large glass dish decorated with sprigs of mint.

Plum Pyramid

This is easier to handle if you make the meringue mixture in two batches. Use half to make the largest and smallest meringue rounds, then use the second batch to make the two middle rounds.

Make sure you don't overcook the plums. They must'nt get mushy.

10 egg whites
575 g / 1¼ lb caster sugar
FILLING
1.5 kg / 3 lb plums
50 g / 2 oz sugar
4 tablespoons water
1.15 litres / 2 pints double cream
50 ml / 2 fl oz brandy or Kirsch

Whisk the egg whites until they stand in stiff peaks, then gradually whisk in the sugar, adding it slowly and whisking with an electric mixer on the highest speed. When all the sugar is incorporated, continue whisking hard until the meringue is very glossy and stiff.

Line four baking trays with non-stick cooking parchment. Draw a circle on each – one 25 cm / 10 in, one 20 cm / 8 in, one 15 cm / 6 in, and one 10 cm / 4 in. Spread the meringue thickly in these circles, then dry out in a very cool oven (110c, 225f, gas ¼), leaving the oven door slightly ajar. The meringues will take about 5 hours to dry out.

For the filling, peel and halve the plums, put them in a pan with the sugar and water, then poach gently until the juice runs and the fruit is just soft but still whole. Leave to cool, then strain the plums, reserving the syrup. Whip the cream with the plum syrup and the brandy or Kirsch, then fold in the fruit. Stack the meringue rounds, sandwiching them together with the plum cream. Spread the remaining cream on top.

Late Night Supper for 20

Jellied Vegetable Mould
Cheese and Nut Stick

*

Chocolate Fudge Cake

*

Iced Herb Tea

A Time Guide

The day before	Make the vegetable mould. Make the fudge cake. Make the nut bread.

•

On the day, well in advance	Decorate the cake. Make the herb tea and chill. Turn out the vegetable mould. Prepare the table.

•

As late as you can leave it	Garnish the mould, then chill.

•

Just before you eat	Remove the vegetable mould from the refrigerator. Put the bread in the oven.

Jellied Vegetable Mould

1 large cauliflower
4–6 large carrots
225 g/8 oz shelled fresh peas
2 red peppers
1 small head celery
2 small red onions
packet of bean sprouts
1 (411 g/14½ oz) can beef consommé
150 ml/¼ pint dry sherry
15 g/½ oz gelatine
450 ml/¾ pint hot water
large bunch of parsley, chopped
handful of small basil leaves
TO SERVE
300 ml/½ pint mayonnaise
4 tablespoons soured cream
2 tablespoons capers, chopped
juice of ½ lemon
salt and pepper

Cook the cauliflower and carrots by steaming them separately for 5 to 10 minutes so that they are only *just* tender. Cook the peas in boiling water for 2 minutes, drain thoroughly. Cut the tops off the peppers, remove the seeds and chop. Slice the celery. Thinly slice the onions. Blanch the pepper and celery together in boiling water for 2 minutes, then drain thoroughly. Wash and dry the bean sprouts. Mix or layer all these vegetables in a glass serving bowl, packing them in well.

Mix the consommé with the sherry. Soften the gelatine in a little cold water, then dissolve over low heat. Stir the gelatine and hot water into the consommé mixture. Sprinkle the parsley and basil over the vegetables and pour in the consommé, then chill thoroughly.

For the sauce, mix the mayonnaise with the cream, capers, lemon juice and seasoning.

Cheese and Nut Stick

1 large, long wholemeal French loaf
225 g/8 oz cream cheese
1 large clove garlic, crushed
some mixed fresh herbs
225 g/8 oz mixed nuts (include at least 50 g/2 oz salted peanuts)
50 g/2 oz butter

Cut the loaf horizontally in half, then place the halves on pieces of cooking foil. Beat the cream cheese with the garlic. Add the herbs to the cheese with seasoning and beat well. Spread this over the cut bread, making a thick, even layer.

Chop the nuts, then press them on top of the cream cheese mixture and dot with the butter. Wrap the loaves completely in foil and bake in a hot oven (220c, 425f, gas 7) for 15 minutes. Serve cut into slices – best hot or warm.

Chocolate Fudge Cake

MAKE TWO OF THESE
225 g/8 oz butter
225 g/8 oz dark soft brown sugar
3 eggs, lightly beaten
1 (400 g/14.1 oz) can condensed milk
25 g/1 oz cocoa
4–5 tablespoons boiling water
275 g/10 oz plain flour
2 teaspoons baking powder
½ teaspoon bicarbonate of soda
DECORATION
150 ml/¼ pint double cream
frosted rose petals and violets

Cream the butter with the sugar until very soft. Beat in the eggs and condensed milk. Dissolve the cocoa in the boiling water, then beat it into the mixture.

Sift the flour with the baking powder and the bicarbonate of soda, then fold this into the mixture. Line and grease a 20 cm/8 in deep cake tin and turn the mixture into it. Bake in a moderate oven (180c, 350f, gas 4) for 1¼ to 1½ hours or until a skewer inserted into the cake comes out clean. Leave the cake in the tin for a few minutes, then turn out on to a wire rack to cool.

Whip the cream until it stands in soft peaks, then swirl over the top of the cake. Add crystallised flowers.

Iced Herb Tea

Make your favourite herb tea (Green Gunpowder iced tea or Lapsang Souchong tea is nice). Add a little sugar (if you must), then cool and strain. Chill the tea thoroughly before serving with lots of ice, slices of lemon and small sprigs of mint.

Brunch Party for 20

Smoked Trout Mousse
*
Fresh Vegetable Gratin
Watercress Salad
*
Lemon Jelly
*
Coffee

A Time Guide

The day before	Make the mousse in lemons and chill. Prepare the gratin ready to put in the oven, then chill. Make the lemon jelly and chill.

●

Two hours before	Turn out the jelly. Lay the table.

●

One hour before	Prepare everything for coffee. Garnish the mousse in lemons.

●

About 45 minutes before	Prepare the oven for the gratin, ready to put it in just before serving the first course. If this is being served outside, find a shady spot and put food out at the last minute. Put out a basket of sun hats for guests.

Smoked Trout Mousse

For a party of twenty make three lots of this rather than trying to prepare vast quantities all at once. The quantities given here are enough to fill about six or eight lemons. Remember to save all the juice from the lemons to make the dessert jelly.

3 whole smoked trout
150 ml / ¼ pint mayonnaise
8 lemons
2 eggs, separated
salt and pepper
15 g / ½ oz gelatine
3 tablespoons water
about 6 nasturtium flowers or leaves

Beside each lemon place a small selection of different types of breads or toasted granary bread cut in strips.

Skin, bone and flake the smoked trout then put it in a food processor or liquidiser with the mayonnaise, the grated rind of 1 lemon, the egg yolks, seasoning to taste and a little lemon juice. Process until smooth.

Dissolve the gelatine in the water. Roughly chop the nasturtium leaves and add them to the mousse, then stir in the gelatine. Whisk the egg whites until stiff, fold these into the mousse and chill until it just begins to set. Meanwhile, carefully cut the tops off the remaining lemons and squeeze out all the juice. Scrape out the lemon shells, taking care not to make any holes in them. Cut a sliver off the base of each lemon so that they stand up neatly.

Spoon the mousse into the lemons, piling it up in the middle. Use old egg boxes to support the lemons while you do this, put them in the refrigerator so that they are thoroughly chilled and the mousse is set before serving. Serve on saucers covered with more leaves.

Fresh Vegetable Gratin

Use all the fresh vegetables you have in the garden, or the freshest you can buy in the shops for this gratin – make it full of colour.

1 cauliflower
450 g / 1 lb small onions (pickling onions)

| 450 g/1 lb baby carrots |
| 450 g/1 lb French beans |
| 450 g/1 lb small new potatoes |
| 450 g/1 lb small tomatoes, halved |
| 450 g/1 lb shelled fresh peas and mange-tout peas |

(Use any vegetables you particularly like – celery, chicory, artichoke bottoms, courgettes, peppers or aubergines are all excellent in this dish. The above is just to give you a guide.)

SAUCE

| 1 large onion, chopped |
| 50 g/2 oz butter |
| 50 g/2 oz flour |
| salt and pepper |
| 300 ml/½ pint dry white wine |
| 300 ml/½ pint milk |
| freshly grated nutmeg |
| 175 g/6 oz Cheddar cheese, grated |
| 300 ml/½ pint double cream |
| 2 eggs, beaten |
| large bunch of parsley, chopped |

Prepare the vegetables according to their type, breaking the cauliflower into pieces, trimming and scraping the root vegetables, trimming beans and mange-tout and cutting any large vegetables into chunks. Steam the vegetables very briefly so that they are still crisp and fresh.

Put the vegetables in one or two ovenproof dishes. To make the sauce, cook the onion in the butter until it is soft but not browned. Stir in the flour and seasoning, then gradually add the wine and the milk. Bring to the boil, stirring all the time, and cook for 2 minutes. Remove the pan from the heat and stir in plenty of nutmeg and most of the cheese, saving some to sprinkle over the top. When the cheese has melted, beat in the cream and eggs, then add the parsley. Taste the sauce to make sure that it is well seasoned, then pour it over the vegetables.

Sprinkle the reserved cheese over the gratin and cook in a moderately hot oven (200c, 400f, gas 6) for about 30 minutes, until golden brown and bubbling. Serve as soon as possible.

Watercress Salad

10 bunches watercress
2 bunches spring onions
1 head curly endive, trimmed and roughly shredded
DRESSING
150 ml / ¼ pint olive oil
4 tablespoons red wine vinegar
2 tablespoons honey
2 tablespoons Worcestershire sauce
grated rind and juice of 2 oranges

Trim the watercress, then put it in a big bowl with the chopped spring onions and the endive. Mix thoroughly. Shake all the dressing ingredients together in a large screw-topped jar, then pour this over the salad just before it is served.

Lemon Jelly

2.25 litres / 4 pints water
75 g / 3 oz gelatine
4 vanilla pods
a few sprigs of lemon balm
juice of 20 lemons (reserved from making the mousse)
grated rind of 4 lemons
450 g / 1 lb sugar
150 ml / ¼ pint Madeira

Pour about 150 ml / ¼ pint of the water on to the gelatine and set aside. Gently heat the rest of the water with the split vanilla pods and lemon balm until it reaches boiling point. Leave to cool, strain and pour back into the pan.

Add the lemon juice and rind, and sugar to the water and heat until the sugar dissolves. Leave to cool. Dissolve the gelatine in the water over low heat. Stir it into the lemon mixture. Add the Madeira and pour into three 1.75 litre / 3 pint moulds. Chill until set, then turn out and decorate with sprigs of lemon balm and flowers.

Breakfasts and Brunches

There are those who ignore breakfast, those who loathe it and those who cannot face the day without it.

If you have friends staying and don't want to be tied to the kitchen stove from the moment you wake up, then try having your special meal in the evening, let everyone sleep late (including yourself) and settle for brunch. By combining breakfast and lunch you can save yourself a great deal of work.

Here are my ideas for some brunches to satisfy the breakfast addicts.

A Victorian Salmon Soufflé
Serves 8

1 kg/2 lb fresh salmon
300 ml/½ pint double cream
2 teaspoons horseradish sauce
6 egg whites
salt and pepper
2 tablespoons chopped chives or a little dill weed

Remove the skin and bones from the salmon. Cut the flesh into cubes and purée it in a liquidiser or food processor with the cream and horseradish sauce. Chill for 15 minutes. Lightly whisk two of the egg whites and beat them into the mixture. Season to taste, then chill until the soufflé is to be cooked (the mixture will keep for up to 6 hours).

Set the oven at moderately hot (200c, 400f, gas 6). Stiffly whisk the rest of the egg whites and fold them into the salmon mixture with the chives or dill weed. Grease a 1.15 litre/2 pint soufflé dish and spoon the mixture into it. Stand the soufflé dish in a roasting tin half filled with hot water and bake in the heated oven for 50 to 60 minutes. When cooked the soufflé should be slightly soft in the centre. Serve with a Hollandaise Sauce (see Vegetable Terrine, page 67) to which some peeled cooked shrimps have been added.

Smoked Salmon with Scrambled Eggs
Serves 6

12 large eggs
salt
cayenne pepper
50 g/2 oz butter
175 g/6 oz smoked salmon pieces or trimmings, chopped

Beat the eggs lightly with a little salt and cayenne to taste. Melt the butter in a large, heavy-based saucepan. Add the egg mixture and cook very slowly, stirring constantly, until the mixture is just beginning to set. Stir in the smoked salmon and serve immediately with brown bread and butter.

Three Fish Kedgeree
Serves 6

100 g/4 oz butter

450 g/1 lb white or brown rice, cooked

1 teaspoon curry powder (or to taste)

175 g/6 oz peeled cooked prawns

100 g/4 oz cooked smoked haddock, free from skin
  and bone, and flaked

225 g/8 oz cooked monkfish, cod or trout, flaked
  (free from skin and bone)

4 hard-boiled eggs, quartered

dash of cream (optional)

2 tablespoons chopped chives

salt and pepper

Heat the butter in a large heavy-based saucepan. Stir
in the rice and curry powder and cook over a low
heat until heated through. Stir in the prawns, smoked
haddock and white fish or trout. Cover and leave over
a very low heat until the fish is hot.

Stir in the eggs, cream (if used) and chives, then
taste the mixture and adjust the seasoning. Serve
immediately.

Superb Fish Cakes with Spicy Sauce
Serves 4 to 6

450 g/1 lb fresh salmon or crab

½ onion, sliced

1 tablespoon vinegar

1 bay leaf

4 peppercorns

salt and pepper

225 g/8 oz potatoes

2 egg yolks

1 tablespoon tomato ketchup

1 teaspoon anchovy essence (optional)

3 tablespoons flour, seasoned

1 egg, beaten

175 g/6 oz fresh white breadcrumbs

oil for shallow frying

TO SERVE

Home-made Tomato Sauce (page 80)

Tabasco sauce to taste

1 bag salted crisps

Put the salmon in a saucepan. Add water to cover, the onion slices, vinegar, bay leaf, peppercorns and a generous pinch of salt. Cover and bring to the boil, then reduce the heat and simmer gently for 5 minutes. Turn off the heat and let the salmon cool in the liquid (or flake the crabmeat).

Meanwhile, boil the potatoes until tender. Drain thoroughly and mash until smooth. Drain and flake the cooled fish, removing all the skin and bones, then mix the fish into the potatoes with the egg yolks, tomato ketchup, anchovy essence and seasoning to taste.

Divide the mixture into 8 portions and shape each into a round cake. Coat the fish cakes in seasoned flour, then dip them in the beaten egg and finally roll them in breadcrumbs. Chill or freeze until ready to cook.

Heat a little oil in a heavy-based frying pan and shallow fry the fish cakes for about 4 minutes on each side, until crisp and golden brown. Drain on absorbent kitchen paper.

To serve, heat the tomato sauce and add Tabasco to taste. Crush the crisps slightly and tip them on to a heated serving plate. Arrange the fish cakes on top and serve the sauce separately.

Turkey Hash
Serves 4 to 6

4 tablespoons oil

2 large onions, thinly sliced

675 g/1½ lb cooked turkey, cut into strips

1 clove garlic, crushed (optional)

4 sticks celery, cut into strips

1 green pepper, deseeded and cut into strips

1 red pepper, deseeded and cut into strips

1 yellow pepper, deseeded and cut into strips

300 ml / ½ pint soured cream

salt and pepper

1 beetroot, cooked, peeled and cut into strips

lemons slices, to garnish

Heat the oil in a large heavy-based frying pan, add the onions and fry until golden brown. Stir in the turkey and garlic (if used) with the celery and peppers, and stir-fry for several minutes to lightly cook the vegetables. Stir in the soured cream and seasoning to taste. Allow to heat through, then carefully stir in the beetroot. Serve immediately garnished, if you like, with slices of lemon.

Summer Chicken Hash Salad
Serves 4 to 6

450 g / 1 lb small new potatoes, cooked

4 cooked chicken breasts

½ cucumber, roughly chopped

2 red peppers, deseeded and roughly chopped

bunch of spring onions, chopped

handful of herbs of your choice, chopped

(tarragon or lemon balm are good)

DRESSING

150 ml ¼ pint mayonnaise

150 ml ¼ pint soured cream

salt and pepper

1 tablespoon toasted sesame seeds

If the potatoes are large then cut them into quarters or chunks. Cut the chicken into chunks, discarding any skin and bone. Add the cucumber and peppers, then toss these ingredients together in a big bowl, adding the spring onions and herbs. Mix all the dressing ingredients and toss them into the salad so that it is well coated.

If the weather turns cold, this salad can be quickly transformed into a delicious chicken hash. Melt some butter or heat a little sunflower oil in large frying pan. Turn the salad (without the dressing) into the pan and press the ingredients down well with the back of a spatula. Cook until the underneath is lightly browned, dot with butter and cook under a hot grill until golden on top. Serve hot, cut into wedges, and offer the dressing with the hash, like a sauce.

Sandwich Soufflé
Serves 6

This dish is better if you prepare it in advance so that the egg and milk mixture has really soaked into the bread.

18 slices bread
75 g/3 oz butter
225 g/8 oz ricotta cheese
large bunch of mixed fresh herbs, chopped
salt and pepper
175 g/6 oz Cheddar cheese, sliced
100 g/4 oz cooked ham, sliced
175 g/6 oz Wensleydale cheese
1 large red pepper
3 eggs
300 ml ½ pint milk
extra Cheddar cheese, grated, for topping

Cut the crusts off the bread if you like, then butter the slices. Beat the ricotta with the herbs and seasoning to taste. Sandwich six slices of the bread and butter together with the ricotta and herbs and another six with the Cheddar cheese and ham.

Crumble the white cheese. Cut the top off the pepper, remove the seeds and chop the shell, then mix this with the crumbled cheese. Sandwich the remaining bread and butter together with this mixture. Press all the sandwiches together firmly, cut in half or quarters.

Beat the eggs with the milk and seasoning. Put the sandwiches in a greased ovenproof dish. Pour the egg and milk over the top and leave to soak for at least an hour. Dot with any remaining butter and sprinkle with the grated Cheddar. Bake in a moderately hot oven (190C, 375F, gas 5) for about 40 to 45 minutes, until golden and set. Serve at once.

Breakfast Kebabs

For a brunch party allow 2 kebabs per person   Serves 4

BACON SPECIALS

| 12 rindless rashers streaky bacon |
| 100 g/4 oz button mushrooms |
| 8 prunes (those which do not require pre-soaking) |
| 100 g/4 oz Gruyère or Edam cheese |
| a little oil |

Roll up the bacon rashers; wipe and trim the mushrooms, then remove the stones from the prunes. Cut
the cheese into eight cubes and press a cube of cheese
in the centre of each prune.

Thread the bacon, mushrooms and prunes on to
four skewers. Brush the kebabs with a little oil
and cook under a hot grill for about 5 minutes,
turning frequently, or until the bacon is crisp and
golden brown.

Note: These kebabs can be prepared in advance and
chilled ready for cooking next day.

SKEWERED AVOCADO WITH SAUSAGE AND BACON

Makes
4 Kebabs

| 2 firm (but ripe) avocado pears |
| 1 tablespoon oil |
| 1 tablespoon lemon juice |
| cayenne pepper *or* Tabasco sauce |
| 14 rindless rashers streaky bacon |
| 12 cocktail sausages |

Peel and stone the avocados, then cut each one into
eight chunks. Mix the oil, lemon juice and cayenne
or Tabasco and brush this mixture over the avocado
chunks. Stretch the bacon with the back of a knife.
Cut each rasher in half and wrap all the avocado
chunks and cocktail sausages individually in a piece
of bacon. Thread the prepared rolls alternately on

to four skewers, beginning and ending each skewer with avocado rolls. Cook the kebabs under a hot grill, turning frequently for about 5 minutes, or until golden brown and thoroughly cooked.

Ham and Cheese on Toast
Serves 4 to 6

Allow 1 slice each of bread and lean cooked ham per person
CHEESE SAUCE
4 tablespoons butter
4 tablespoons flour
250 ml/8 fl oz milk
salt and pepper
1 egg yolk
225 g/8 oz Gruyère or Cheddar cheese, grated
GARNISH
tomato slices
sprigs of parsley

Toast the slices of bread and place a slice of ham on each. To make the sauce, melt the butter in a pan and stir in the flour. Add the milk and whisk over a medium heat until smooth and boiling. Add salt, pepper and the egg yolk. Stir until thoroughly mixed, then remove from the heat. Add the grated cheese and stir until it has melted.

Pour the cheese mixture over the slices of toast and ham and place them under a hot grill until golden brown. Garnish each portion with a slice of tomato and parsley.

Beef and Rice 'Lasagne'
Serves 6

2 tablespoons oil
2 onions, finely chopped
2 cloves garlic, crushed (or to taste)
1 kg/2 lb chuck steak, minced
1 kg/2 lb tomatoes, peeled, quartered and deseeded
2 tablespoons Worcestershire sauce (or to taste)

3 tablespoons tomato purée (or to taste)
1 beef stock cube
salt and pepper
50 g/2 oz butter
50 g/2 oz flour
600 ml/1 pint milk
225 g/8 oz cheese (Cheddar, Gruyère or similar), grated
450 g/1 lb cooked long-grain rice (brown or white)

Heat the oil in a large heavy-based saucepan; cook the onions and garlic slowly until soft. Add the beef and stir-fry over high heat until browned. Reduce the heat and stir in the tomatoes, Worcestershire sauce, purée, stock cube and seasoning. Simmer gently, stirring frequently, for 15 minutes.

Another recipe that children like a lot!

Make a cheese sauce by melting the butter in a saucepan, stir in the flour, then gradually add the milk, stirring continuously, until smooth. Bring to the boil, stirring continuously, and cook until thick and smooth. Season to taste and stir in 175 g/6 oz of the grated cheese.

Spread half of the meat mixture in a greased large oblong shallow ovenproof baking dish. Cover with the cooked rice, then the remaining meat mixture. Spoon the cheese sauce on top and sprinkle with the remaining cheese. Bake in a moderate oven (180C, 350F, gas 4) for 30 to 40 minutes, until golden and bubbling.

Turkey Lasagne
Serves 8

A different way to eat up leftover turkey.

1 kg/2 lb cooked, boneless turkey meat, minced or chopped
1 red pepper, deseeded and cut into fine strips
100 g/4 oz blanched almonds, toasted or fried
175 g/6 oz lasagne verdi sheets (those which do not require pre-cooking)
100 g/4 oz mozzarella cheese, thinly sliced

SAUCE
75 g / 3 oz butter
40 g / 1½ oz flour
600 ml / 1 pint milk
½ teaspoon mustard powder, or to taste
juice from crushing 1 clove garlic
100 g / 4 oz Gruyère or Cheddar cheese, grated
salt and pepper

Grease a large oblong shallow ovenproof baking dish. Mix the turkey with the red pepper and the almonds.

Make the sauce: melt the butter in a large saucepan, stir in the flour, then gradually mix in the milk. Bring to the boil, stirring constantly, until smooth and quite thick. Simmer for a minute.

Remove the saucepan from the heat, and stir in the mustard, garlic juice, cheese and seasoning to taste. Stir the turkey mixture into the sauce and spoon a layer of it into the prepared dish, then cover with a layer of lasagne. Continue layering up the lasagne and sauce in this way until all the ingredients have been used, finishing with a layer of the sauce mixture. Top with the mozzarella cheese, then bake in a moderate oven (180C, 350F, gas 4) for 40 to 45 minutes, or until golden brown.

Egg in a Bun
Serves 6

6 granary buns or crisp breakfast rolls
50 g / 2 oz butter, softened
75 g / 3 oz rindless rashers bacon, cooked and crumbled
3 eggs
225 g / 8 oz Gruyère cheese, grated

Scoop out the middle of each bun, then butter the inside of each one and stand them on a baking tray. Bake in a moderate oven (180C, 350F, gas 4) for about 5 minutes, then remove from the oven and place a little of the bacon inside each bun.

Crack an egg into each bun and sprinkle the grated cheese on top, then return to the oven for 15 to 20 minutes, or until the egg is cooked to taste. Serve immediately.

Variation

Egg in Tomato: Allow 1 large beef steak tomato and 1 egg per person. Cut the top off the tomato and scoop out the middle, then leave the shell to drain for a few minutes (upside-down on absorbent kitchen paper). Break an egg into the tomato shell, add seasoning and 1 tablespoon single cream, then top with grated cheese. Bake as above and serve immediately, with triangles of fried bread if you like.

Sensational Brunch

For three or four people use six to eight eggs. Peel and thinly slice one large tomato, slice two or three mushrooms and chop a couple of spring onions. Put the vegetables in a pot, season and cook lightly. Grate some Cheddar cheese into a non-stick saucepan and melt it slowly, then break the eggs into it. When the whites start to set, stir and dump in the warm vegetables. Stir continuously until the whole slop sets, then serve it on toast.

Spinach Soufflé
Serves 4 to 6

100 ml / 4 fl oz mayonnaise
50 g / 2 oz plain flour
300 ml / ½ pint milk
100 g / 4 oz Cheddar cheese, grated
salt and pepper
275 g / 10 oz thoroughly drained, cooked spinach
4 egg yolks, lightly beaten
5 egg whites

Try using cooked brocc'li instead of spinach, chopping it in the food processor first.

First prepare a 1.75 litre/3 pint soufflé dish. Butter the dish and tie a wide band of double thickness greaseproof paper around the outside. It should be high enough to stand at least 7.5 cm/3 in above the rim of the dish. Secure the band in place with a piece of sticky tape and string.

Combine the mayonnaise with the flour in a saucepan, then gradually add the milk and stir over a low heat until the mixture thickens. Off the heat, stir in the grated cheese, seasoning and cooked spinach. Mix in the egg yolks. Whisk the egg whites until they stand in stiff peaks, then fold them into the soufflé.

Turn into the prepared dish and bake in a moderate oven (160c, 325f, gas 3) for about 40 to 60 minutes, or until the soufflé is well risen. To serve, carefully remove the paper collar: do this by easing it away from the mixture with the blade of a long knife. Serve immediately.

Alsace Onion Tarts
Serves 8

8 individual pastry shells
4 tablespoons oil
450 g / 1 lb strong onions, chopped
1 bay leaf
sprig of fresh thyme
salt and pepper
150 ml / ¼ pint dry Alsatian wine
2 eggs
200 ml / 7 fl oz single cream

Prepare and cook the pastry shells according to the recipe instructions.

Heat the oil in a non-stick frying pan. Add the onions, bay leaf, thyme and seasoning, then cover and cook gently until the onions are soft and transparent. Add the wine and simmer, uncovered, until all the liquid has evaporated. Remove the bay leaf and thyme and taste for seasoning. Whisk the eggs and cream together.

Divide the onions between the quiche shells and pour in the egg mixture. Place on a heated baking sheet and bake in a moderately hot oven (190c, 375f, gas 5) for 15 minutes. Serve hot or cold.

Bread and Cheese Brunch
Serves 6

15 g / ½ oz butter
8 slices bread, crusts removed
450 g / 1 lb Cheddar cheese, grated
600 ml / 1 pint milk
3 eggs
1 teaspoon dried sage
salt and pepper

Line the base of a buttered ovenproof dish with half the bread, then sprinkle half the cheese on top in a thick layer. Top with the remaining bread and sprinkle the rest of the cheese on top.

Beat the milk, eggs, sage and seasoning together, then pour this mixture over the bread and cheese and leave in the refrigerator for a few hours (or overnight) so that the liquid really soaks into the bread.

Bake in a moderate oven (180C, 350F, gas 4) for 1 hour, until crisp and golden. Serve immediately.

The Alternative Sandwich
Serves 6

1 large unsliced loaf

TURKEY FILLING

225 g / 8 oz cooked turkey, finely chopped
2 sticks celery
75 g / 3 oz light cream cheese
3 tablespoons mayonnaise
1 teaspoon Dijon mustard
salt and pepper

Smoked Chicken is a nice alternative to the turkey.

CHEESE AND WATERCRESS FILLING

1 bunch watercress, trimmed and very finely chopped
75 g / 3 oz crumbled blue cheese
75 g / 3 oz Cheddar cheese, grated
2 tablespoons mayonnaise
1 tablespoon finely chopped walnuts

HAM FILLING

75 g/3 oz cream cheese
3 tablespoons mayonnaise
75 g/3 oz lean cooked ham, finely chopped
1 tablespoon finely chopped parsley

Mix the ingredients for the different fillings in separate bowls, cover and set aside. Remove all the crusts from the loaf and cut the bread horizontally into four thick slices.

Spread each of three slices thickly with one of the filling mixtures, then sandwich the slices back together again and top with the fourth slice of bread. Sprinkle with chopped herbs and wrap the loaf tightly in cling film. Chill in the refrigerator for a few hours, then serve cut into slices, with your favourite chutney as an accompaniment.

Home-made Cereal
Serves 2

4 handfuls oatmeal
1 large handful desiccated coconut
1 small handful mixed nuts
1 tablespoon sunflower seeds
1 tablespoon bran
50 g/2 oz demerara sugar
2 teaspoons clear honey

Mix all the ingredients and spread the cereal evenly in a lightly oiled baking tin. Bake in a moderate oven (180c, 350f, gas 4) until brown and crunchy, stirring it up every few minutes. Cool and store in an airtight jar.

Eat with yogurt or milk, for breakfast, or on its own as a snack while waiting for the turkey to cook. You could also give it to a health-conscious friend in a pretty jar as a gift.

leave in ?
the to
gas

| 100 g/4 oz butter |
| 225 g/8 oz soft brown sugar |
| 1 egg |
| 2 ripe bananas, mashed |
| 225 g/8 oz plain flour |
| 1 teaspoon salt |
| 1½ teaspoons baking powder |
| 4 tablespoons natural yogurt |

*uld ʔIS
Proof!*

Beat the butter and sugar together
beat in the egg. Mix in the mash
together the flour, salt and baking p   mix half
the yogurt into the creamed butter and sugar, then
add half the flour mixture. Next mix in the rest of
the yogurt and finally the rest of the flour.

Grease a 450 g/1 lb loaf tin, turn the bread mixture
into it and bake in a moderate oven (180C, 350F,
gas 4) for 1 hour, or until the loaf sounds hollow
when tapped on the underside. Leave to cool on a
wire rack.

Quick Walnut Bread

Makes two
1 kg/2 lb
loaves

| 1.4 kg/3 lb wholemeal flour |
| ½ teaspoon salt |
| 25 g/1 oz fresh yeast *or* 15 g/½ oz dried yeast |
| 1 litre/1¾ pints lukewarm water |
| 1½ teaspoons honey |
| 175 g/6 oz walnuts, chopped |

Mix the flour with the salt in a large, warmed mixing
bowl. Mix the yeast with a third of the water and the
honey. Leave in a warm place for about 10 minutes,
or until frothy. Gradually work the yeast liquid into
the flour with the remaining water, adding a little
more water if necessary, to make a soft but not sticky
dough. Knead thoroughly for 5 minutes or until the
dough is smooth and elastic. Knead in the walnuts.

Divide the dough in half and shape each piece into
a loaf. Place in greased 1 kg/2 lb loaf tins, cover and

warm place until the dough has risen to
p of each tin. Bake in a hot oven (230c, 450F,
8) for 5 minutes, then reduce the temperature to
(200c, 400F, gas 6) and bake for a further 30 minutes
or until the bread sounds hollow when tapped on the
underside. Leave to cool on a wire rack.
Note: This bread can be frozen.

Breakfast Muffins

Makes
12 to 15

150 g/5 oz self-raising flour
100 g/4 oz wholemeal flour
100 g/4 oz muesli
100 g/4 oz soft brown sugar
3 teaspoons baking powder
¼ teaspoon salt
1 egg, beaten
300 ml/½ pint milk
50 ml/2 fl oz sunflower oil
75 g/3 oz raisins

Stir the flours, muesli, sugar, baking powder and salt
together in a large mixing bowl and make a well
in the middle. In another bowl beat all the liquid
ingredients together, then pour them into the flour
mixture. Gradually mix the dry and liquid ingredients
together and fold in the raisins. Mix thoroughly.

Spoon the mixture into 12 or 15 greased muffin tins,
leaving a small space at the top of each tin. Bake in a
moderately hot oven (200c, 400F, gas 6) for 20 to 25
minutes or until golden brown.

Allow the muffins to cool slightly in their tins before
turning them out on to a wire rack. Serve while still
warm with butter and honey.

Try a handful of walnuts or any crunchy health food cereal instead of muesli, or use chopped prunes, apples, bananas or apricots instead of raisins. Let the children make these because whatever they do this recipe never fails.

A Great Bread without Yeast

Makes a
medium loaf

450 g / 1 lb wholemeal flour	
a couple of handfuls of kibbled wheat	
1 teaspoon salt	
25 g / 1 oz butter	
2 teaspoons bicarbonate of soda	
2 teaspoons cream of tartar	
100 g / 4 oz mixed nuts, finely chopped	
400 ml / 14 fl oz soured cream (or buttermilk if you prefer)	

Put the flour in a bowl with the wheat and salt. Rub in the butter, then add the bicarbonate of soda and the cream of tartar. Stir in the nuts and soured cream to make a soft dough.

Knead the dough lightly, shape it into a round and flatten it slightly on a greased baking tray. Cut a deep cross in the top and bake the bread in a moderately hot oven (200C, 400F, gas 6) for 30 minutes, or until the bread sounds hollow when tapped on the underside. Leave the loaf to cool on a wire rack.

Note: This bread freezes well, so make a few loaves when you have the time. Use other sorts of nuts and seeds or grains in the dough to make the loaves different.

Lazy Breakfast or Brunch

A nice way of presenting a late Sunday breakfast (or brunch) is to take a long, flattish basket, line it with leaves (Virginia creeper is always useful for this) and make small piles of different things — rather like an artist's palette — on it. Heap up piles of dried bananas, apricots. Add bunches of black and green grapes, some fresh figs and nectarines, strings of redcurrants and blackcurrants. Add some shelled nuts and flowers.

Put in the middle of the table, with some cheese, some Ginger Thins (page 213) or muffins and a large pot of coffee and fresh orange juice.

Pick-Me-Up Breakfast

Put into the liquidiser 300 ml / ½ pint chilled milk, 1 egg, 1 banana (cut up), honey to taste and grated nutmeg. Whirl until frothy, pour into a tall glass.

Energy Breakfast

Dissolve 2 lemon-flavoured Vitamin C tablets in 100 ml / 4 fl oz orange juice and pour into a liquidiser or food processor. Add 250 ml / 8 fl oz skimmed milk, 1 peeled and stoned peach, 2 teaspoons clear honey and some freshly grated nutmeg and blend until well mixed. Pour into a tall glass to serve.

Courgette Bread

For breakfast serve warmed bread, thickly sliced, with a selection of marmalades or jams. The courgette bread freezes well and it can be defrosted quickly in either the microwave oven or in the conventional oven.

Makes a
1 kg/2 lb loaf

225 g/8 oz plain flour (or half plain, half wholemeal)
1½ teaspoons baking powder
½ teaspoon bicarbonate of soda
1 teaspoon salt
100 g/4 oz butter
225 g/8 oz courgettes, coarsely grated
50 g/2 oz sunflower seeds
grated rind and juice of 1 orange
2 eggs, lightly beaten
small handful of sunflower seeds to sprinkle on top

Put the flour, baking powder, bicarbonate of soda and salt in a bowl then rub in the butter until the mixture looks like fine breadcrumbs. Stir in the courgettes and sunflower seeds. Add the orange rind and juice, stir then add the eggs. Mix well to combine all the ingredients.

Thoroughly grease a 1 kg/2 lb loaf tin and put the mixture in it. Smooth the top slightly, sprinkle with some sunflower seeds and bake in a moderate oven (180c, 350f, gas 4) for about 1½ hours, until well risen and golden on top. Leave the bread to cool on a wire rack.

Instant Jam

Take advantage of all the fruit in season and before going to bed mash either peaches, raspberries, strawberries or blackberries with a little icing sugar. Put in pots and cover with cling film. Leave in the refrigerator overnight and serve with muffins or croissants for breakfast.

Sweet Apple Omelette

Serves 4

This makes a nice breakfast or brunch. If you are having it as a pudding, then serve with Greek yogurt.

5 eggs
4 tablespoons single cream
50 g/2 oz caster sugar
grated rind of 1 lemon
½ teaspoon ground cinnamon
2 tablespoons rum
3–4 tart dessert apples
25 g/1 oz butter
a couple of handfuls of sultanas
1 tablespoon brown sugar

Beat the eggs with the cream, sugar, lemon rind, cinnamon and rum. Peel and core the apples, then slice them into rings. Cook these briefly in the butter in a large omelette pan, turning the slices once and adding the sultanas as soon as they are turned.

Beat the egg mixture thoroughly, pour it into the pan on top of the apples and cook over a moderate heat until it is well set underneath, lifting the edges of the mixture to allow unset egg to run into the pan. Have ready a very hot grill. Sprinkle the omelette with brown sugar, put the pan under the grill and finish cooking the top of the omelette until set and golden.

Serve the omelette freshly cooked, cut into wedges.

Away from it all

These are some recipes for when you want to simply pack up some food and get away from it all. And remember, picnics don't have to be the usual dreary sandwiches.

Helpful tips for picnics

- Always take mosquito spray and sting cream, also food covers (the best ones are umbrella shaped and open out quite large)
- Take face cloths soaked in cold water scented with cologne and packed in ice-filled polythene bags.
- Take sun hats and (dare I say it) a large umbrella.

Salad in a Loaf
Serves 6

1 wholemeal sandwich loaf
75 g/3 oz butter
450 g/1 lb cooked ham in one piece
6 hard-boiled eggs
2 tablespoons capers
175 g/6 oz tiny shelled broad beans (blanched briefly if you think they need it)
bunch of chives, chopped
50 g/2 oz stoned black olives, chopped
DRESSING
300 ml ½ pint mayonnaise
1 tablespoon mustard with horseradish
2 teaspoons chopped tarragon
pinch of sugar
salt and pepper
1 clove garlic, crushed (optional)
a few drops of lemon juice

Thinly slice all the crusts off the loaf. Horizontally slice a lid off the bread, then cut out all the middle of the loaf leaving about 2.5 cm/1 in of bread all round the sides and base to make a box shape. (You can freeze the bread which is removed from inside the loaf to make breadcrumbs.)

Melt the butter, then brush the loaf and the lid all over, both inside and out. Put the bread on a baking tray and bake in a moderately hot oven (200C, 400F, gas 6) for about 20 minutes or until crisp and browned. Leave to cool.

Cut the ham into cubes. Quarter the eggs and mix them with the ham, capers, beans, chives and olives. Lightly toss the ingredients, then put the salad in a plastic bag and put this inside the crisp loaf and put the lid on top. Wrap the whole loaf in foil or cling film and chill it until you are ready to leave.

Mix all the ingredients for the dressing in a container with a tight-fitting lid. Chill. When you arrive simply turn the salad out of the bag into the loaf crust and pour the dressing on the salad. Eat with some of the container loaf.

Three-Melon Salad
Serves 6 to 8

1 watermelon
1 honeydew melon
1 charentais melon
lemon balm or pineapple mint (if you have it)
1 (227 g/8 oz) can lychees, drained

Cut a slice off the top of the watermelon to make a lid. Scoop out all the flesh and cut it into chunks, discarding the seeds. Put the watermelon flesh in a bowl. Halve the honeydew, discard the seeds, then scoop out the flesh and mix it with the watermelon. Do the same with the charentais. (You can use a melon baller for this.)

Add the sprigs of lemon balm or mint and lychees to the melon mixture. Fill the watermelon shell with the melon and wrap it securely in a couple of thicknesses of cling film.

Pack the melon in plenty of ice and it will keep cold for several hours. This is best in a chiller box, otherwise put some ice in a very thick plastic bag, and put the completely sealed melon on top before sealing the bag.

Minted Cucumber Mousse
Serves 6

½ cucumber, lightly peeled and diced
salt and pepper
15 g/½ oz gelatine
150 ml/¼ pint hot chicken stock
large bunch of mint
1 tablespoon white wine vinegar (or cider vinegar)
1½ teaspoons caster sugar
pinch of ground coriander or mace
225 g/8 oz cream cheese
150 ml/¼ pint double cream

This mousse makes a delicious and attractive first course for a dinner party.

Put the cucumber in a sieve or colander over a bowl and sprinkle it with salt, then set aside for 30 minutes. Soften the gelatine in a little cold water, then dissolve in the stock and leave until almost cold.

Chop some of the mint to flavour the mousse. Dry the cucumber. Mix it with the vinegar, sugar, coriander or mace and mint. Beat cheese, adding stock gradually. Then add cucumber. Stir well and leave until beginning to set.

Whip the cream until it is just thick, then fold it into the mousse. Pour into a 23 cm/9 in ring mould. Chill until set.

Wrap the mould completely in cling film or foil to carry on the picnic. Turn it out and fill the middle with watercress or alfalfa sprouts or cucumber.

Chicken Strips
Serves 6

2 or 3 chicken breast fillets
salt and pepper
a little flour
100 g/4 oz dry breadcrumbs
bunch of parsley, chopped
grated rind of 1 lime or lemon
1 egg, beaten
oil for deep frying
TO SERVE
halved lemons

Cut the chicken into fine strips. Season the flour fairly generously, then coat the pieces of chicken in it. Mix the breadcrumbs with the parsley and lime or lemon rind. Put the mixture on a deep plate.

Dip the floured chicken strips in the egg, then roll them in the breadcrumb mixture to coat them completely. Lay a piece of greaseproof paper on a baking tray and put the chicken on it, then (if you have time) put the tray in the freezer for about 15 to 30 minutes.

Heat the oil for deep frying to 190c/375f. Drop the chicken strips in the oil and cook until crisp and golden. Drain thoroughly on absorbent kitchen paper and leave to cool.

To pack the chicken, line a container with some absorbent kitchen paper and put the strips on top. Put lemon halves in the corners and place an airtight lid on top. Or completely wrap in cling film or foil.

Stuffed Mange-tout
Serves 6

As many mange-tout as you can be bothered to fill
FILLING
100 g/4 oz cream cheese
1 tablespoon natural yogurt
salt and pepper
a few spring onions, chopped
50 g/2 oz peeled cooked prawns, finely chopped
2 teaspoons tomato purée

To have with a glass of wine while you unpack your picnic.

Blend all the filling ingredients together. Gently open the mange-tout pods down one side and fill with the mixture. Pack in a container lined with mint.

Note: Steam the mange-tout if you prefer.

Chicken and Grapes
Serves 4

4 small melons
4 chicken breasts, poached
25 g/1 oz sliced blanched almonds, toasted
bunch of spring onions, chopped
225 g/8 oz seedless white grapes
250 ml/8 fl oz mayonnaise
salt and pepper
chopped mint

Cut the tops off the melons and reserve these lids. Scoop out and discard the seeds, then scoop out the melon flesh and cut it into chunks. Cut the chicken into pieces and mix with all the other ingredients together in a big bowl, adding enough mint to flavour but not overpower the salad.

Dry the insides of the melons with absorbent kitchen paper, then fill them with salad and replace the lids. Stick sprigs of mint into the lids if you like and wrap the melons completely in cling film to keep the lids firmly in place. Chill thoroughly before taking on the picnic.

Note: This is a great way of making a wonderful chicken salad which can travel and be served in its own container.

Runner Bean Salad

Try cold runner beans mixed with cottage cheese.

Slice some fresh runner beans and remove any tough strings. Blanch them very briefly in boiling water, then plunge them into ice cold water. Drain thoroughly. Mix the beans with freshly ground black pepper and a squeeze of lemon juice for the best flavour.

Stuffed Courgettes in Lettuce Leaves
Serves 4

4 courgettes
salt and pepper
FILLING
100 g/4 oz cream cheese
1 ripe dessert pear, peeled, cored and chopped
about 8 radishes, trimmed and chopped
a couple of spring onions, chopped
2 tablespoons chopped tarragon
4–8 lettuce leaves

Trim the courgettes, then cut them in half lengthways and scoop out the seeds. Blanch the courgette halves very briefly in boiling salted water, then drain them thoroughly on absorbent kitchen paper.

Beat the cream cheese, add the pear and radishes. Add the spring onions and tarragon with seasoning to taste. Sandwich the courgette halves back together with the filling, then wrap them in one or two lettuce leaves. Pack the courgettes in a container on ice.

Sandwich Loaf

Some sandwiches are definitely boring – here is a way of making a sandwich into something special.

Serves 6 to 8

1 wholemeal sandwich loaf
225 g/8 oz cooked ham
300 ml/½ pint mayonnaise
2 teaspoons green peppercorns (optional)
225 g/8 oz cooked chicken
a few spring onions, chopped
350 g/12 oz cream cheese
large bunch of mixed fresh herbs, chopped

Cut all the crusts off the bread to leave an oblong-shaped loaf, then cut this through horizontally into seven slices. Blend the ham with half the mayonnaise in a liquidiser or food processor until smooth then stir in the peppercorns. In the same way, blend the remaining mayonnaise with the chicken and add the spring onions. Beat the cream cheese with the herbs.

Sandwich the slices of bread together with the three separate fillings so that there are two layers of each. Pack the loaf tightly in cling film and chill it thoroughly.

The loaf should be cut vertically into slices, then reshaped and packed securely in cling film ready to take on the picnic. The slices can be cut across into fingers to make them easier to eat if you like.

Drained canned tuna and chopped hard-boiled egg and some chopped spring onions in mayonnaise (for one layer). Finely chopped watercress and cream cheese (for the next layer). Grated carrot, sultanas and mayonnaise (for the third layer).

Alternative Fillings

White Cabbage Salad

For a delicious, simple-to-prepare salad, mix shredded white cabbage with shredded chicory leaves and finely sliced green pepper. Sprinkle a few caraway seeds over the salad and dress it with mayonnaise thinned with a little single cream or with a vinaigrette dressing if you prefer.

Picnic Croissants

Makes 12

Instead of sandwiches, try filling wholemeal croissants with unusual mixtures.

12 large croissants
CARROT AND NECTARINE FILLING
3–4 carrots, grated
2 nectarines, halved, stoned and chopped
50 g/2 oz walnuts, chopped
salt and pepper
a few drops of lemon juice
4 tablespoons mayonnaise
SUNFLOWER AND CRESS FILLING
1 carton mustard and cress
handful of sunflower seeds, lightly toasted
1 small red onion, sliced into thin rings
1 dessert apple, cored and diced
a few drops of lemon juice
2 tablespoons soured cream

Buy croissants from a good baker. Avoid the thin, limp ones.

Mix the carrots with the nectarines and walnuts, then add seasoning to taste and sprinkle with lemon juice. Mix in the mayonnaise.

For the second filling, mix the cress with the sunflower seeds and onion. Sprinkle the apple with lemon juice and toss well with the mustard and cress. Mix with soured cream and season to taste.

Split the croissants through and fill them with the fillings, then wrap each one in cling film to keep them whole.

Cabbage with Kumquat Dressing

Poach 50 g/2 oz kumquats in 4 tablespoons water and 2 tablespoons red wine vinegar for about 10 minutes, or until tender. Keep the pan covered to retain all the moisture.

Put the kumquats with the cooking liquid in a food processor or liquidiser with the juice of 1 lemon and 150 ml / ¼ pint sunflower oil. Add seasoning to taste and blend until smooth and thick. Stir in 2 tablespoons chopped fresh marjoram and 1 tablespoon finely chopped shallot or onion.

Pour the dressing over finely shredded white or red cabbage just before it is served.

Cheese and Vegetable Terrine
Serves 6 to 8

100 g / 4 oz butter
75 g / 3 oz plain flour
600 ml / 1 pint milk
2 eggs, beaten
225 g / 8 oz carrots, chopped
1 onion, chopped
salt and pepper
225 g / 8 oz ricotta cheese
bunch of watercress, trimmed
½ cauliflower, lightly cooked
75 g / 3 oz white cheese (Lancashire, Caerphilly or Cheshire), crumbled
225 g / 8 oz shelled peas, cooked
some chopped mint

Melt 75 g / 3 oz of the butter in a saucepan, stir in the flour then gradually add the milk and bring to the boil, stirring all the time. Remove from the heat and beat in the eggs, set aside.

Cook the carrots and onion in the remaining butter until the onion is soft. Stir in a quarter of the sauce then put into a liquidiser or food processor and blend until smooth. Add seasoning to taste, then turn the mixture into the prepared tin and smooth the top down well.

Blend the ricotta cheese with the watercress and one-third of the remaining sauce. Season. Line the bake of a 1 kg / 2 lb loaf tin with greaseproof paper and grease well and pour the mixture into tin, pressing down lightly to make an even layer.

Break the cauliflower into small pieces and blend these with the cheese and half the remaining sauce until smooth. Season and turn into the tin to form the third layer, spreading it out evenly.

Finally, blend the peas and mint with the remaining sauce until smooth. Spread this mixture evenly over the cauliflower layer. Stand the terrine in a roasting tin half filled with boiling water. Bake in a moderate oven (160C, 325F, gas 3) for 1½ hours. Leave until completely cold and chill for a few hours before wrapping the whole tin in a double thickness of foil. Turn the terrine out just before you serve it. Garnish with herbs.

Note: If you don't have a chiller box to carry your food in, put as many ice cubes as you can in a dustbin bag, place your containers (well-sealed with foil or cling film) in the bag and tie it very securely. This helps to keep food in good condition. Take the food out carefully and the water might be useful for sticky fingers.

Whole Artichokes Vinaigrette

These are easy to pack and carry on a picnic, with the dressing in a screw-topped jar to pour over the vegetables at the last minute.

To cook artichokes, simply trim the ends of the leaves and put them in boiling salted water — they take about 15 to 20 minutes depending on size and age. Drain and rinse in cold water, then pull out the hairy choke from the middle to leave the outer leaves and the bottom in place. Cool, wrap tightly in cling film and chill.

Larger artichokes can take anything up to 45 minutes to cook.

Make a well-flavoured vinaigrette dressing, with oil of your choice, cider vinegar or wine vinegar, a pinch of sugar and seasoning, some mustard, juice from a clove of garlic (optional) and 2 tablespoons chopped chervil or dill. Shake up the dressing just before you use it.

Pineapple and Mango Salad

Peel and core a large ripe pineapple, then cut into chunks. Peel 3 ripe mangos and cut the flesh off the stones in thin slices. Cut these in half and mix with the pineapple in a container which has a tight-fitting lid. Sprinkle in a few tablespoons of white rum and a little icing sugar if you like. If you have any, a couple of tablespoons of coconut liqueur taste good sprinkled over the fruit but you will definitely have to omit the sugar with this. Chill thoroughly before taking on the picnic.

Note: When tiny pineapples are available, use one per person and cut off the tops. Scoop out the insides and chop the fruit. Mix with thinly sliced kiwi fruit and put back into the pineapple. Put the lid back on top and chill before serving.

Slow Baked Salmon

Serves 8 to 10

1 (about 2.25 kg/5 lb in weight) salmon or salmon trout
50 g/2 oz butter
150 ml/¼ pint dry white wine
bay leaf
bunch of dill sprigs
a few sprigs of tarragon
small bunch of parsley
salt and pepper
dill sprigs to garnish

Ask the fishmonger to clean the fish for you. Take a large, double-thick piece of cooking foil and lay it on a roasting tin – there should be plenty to wrap the salmon. Butter the middle of the foil, put the salmon on it and dot with the remaining butter.

Cup the sides of the foil, sprinkle the wine over the salmon and add the bay leaf. Roughly chop the other herbs and sprinkle over the fish. Add a little seasoning and wrap up securely in the foil.

Bake in a moderate oven (160c, 325f, gas 3) for about 1 hour or until the fish flakes. Check that the salmon is cooked through, then wrap it tightly and leave to cool. Remove the skin from head to tail and wrap the salmon in fresh foil. Add a few sprigs of dill and chill. Serve with home-made mayonnaise.

Stilton and Walnut Drumsticks
Serves 4

8 chicken drumsticks
about 50 g/2 oz butter
salt and pepper
4 bay leaves
sprigs of fresh rosemary
DRESSING
225 g/8 oz blue Stilton cheese
4–6 tablespoons port
4 tablespoons mayonnaise
225 g/8 oz walnuts, finely chopped
150 ml/¼ pint soured cream
2 lettuce hearts, divided into leaves, to serve

Put the drumsticks in a roasting tin with the butter dotted on top. Sprinkle with salt and pepper, then put the bay leaves and rosemary in between the drumsticks. Cook in a moderately hot oven (200C, 400F, gas 6) for about 30 minutes until the drumsticks are quite well browned. Drain them on absorbent kitchen paper and allow to cool.

For the dressing, crumble the cheese, then mash it with the port and mayonnaise. Add the walnuts and stir in the soured cream. Taste and adjust the seasoning; chill the dressing.

To serve, arrange the drumsticks on the leaves from lettuce hearts (this enables you to pick up the drumsticks in a lettuce leaf). Serve the dressing separately.

Savoury Filo Bake
Serves 6

175 g/6 oz Gruyère cheese
2 medium courgettes
2 tablespoons chopped fresh basil
bunch of spring onions, chopped
salt and pepper
8 sheets filo pastry
50 g/2 oz butter, melted

Grate the Gruyère and the courgettes, then mix in the basil, onions and seasoning.

Lay the filo pastry on the work surface brushing each sheet with melted butter as you stack them up.

Spread the filling over the top of the pastry stack, leaving a border, then fold the edges over so that they overlap in the middle. Press together to seal in the filling.

Put on a greased baking tray and brush with more butter. Cook in a moderately hot oven (200c, 400f, gas 6) for 20 to 30 minutes or until the pastry is puffed up and golden. Serve hot or cold.

Fruity Curried Macaroni
Serves 4 to 6

175 g/6 oz short-cut macaroni
salt and pepper
350 g/12 oz cooked ham
3 ripe peaches
3 large dessert apples
juice of 1 lemon
1 small red or white onion
50 g/2 oz roasted almonds
DRESSING
1 tablespoon grated fresh root ginger
1 small onion, chopped
25 g/1 oz butter
3–4 teaspoons curry powder
4 tablespoons each of soured cream and mayonnaise
3 tablespoons mango chutney (optional)

Cook the macaroni in boiling salted water for about 10 minutes or until *just* tender, then drain it thoroughly and rinse in cold water. Leave to drain.

Cut the ham into strips and mix with the macaroni. Put the peaches in a large bowl, cover them with boiling water and leave for about a minute. Remove and use a sharp pointed knife to remove the skin. Cut into slices. Add the peaches to the macaroni.

Core and slice the apples (dip in lemon juice), cut the onion into thin slices and add both to the salad, then toss in the almonds. Make the dressing: cook the ginger and onion in the butter until the onion is soft but not browned. Stir in the curry powder and cook gently for a further 3 to 4 minutes, stirring to prevent it from sticking. Press firmly through a sieve so that you get all the juice and flavour without the bits. Fold into the soured cream and mayonnaise. (You can add mango chutney at this point.) Pour the dressing over the salad, toss well and put it in the refrigerator until it is served.

Roquefort Egg Mousse

Serves 6 to 8

9 eggs
50 g/2 oz butter
50 g/2 oz plain flour
salt and pepper
300 ml/½ pint milk
150 ml/¼ pint double cream
225 g/8 oz Roquefort cheese
handful of chives, chopped
4 teaspoons gelatine
4 tablespoons water
watercress to garnish

Hard-boil 6 eggs, separate the others. Melt the butter in a saucepan, stir in the flour and seasoning and cook for a minute or so. Pour in the milk, stirring all the time, and bring to the boil, still stirring. Cook for a minute until thick and smooth, then remove the pan from the heat and beat in the 3 egg yolks. Add the cream and stir well. Mash the cheese with a little of the sauce, then add it to the rest of the sauce and stir well, until well blended and smooth, or give it a quick whirl in the food processor.

Chop the hard-boiled eggs and stir into the mixture with the chives. Taste and adjust the seasoning if necessary. Soften the gelatine in the water, then dissolve over low heat. When thoroughly dissolved, gently stir the gelatine into the mousse and leave until half set.

Whisk the egg whites until stiff, fold them into the mousse and turn it into a 1.4 litre/2½ pint mould. Chill thoroughly until firm.

To serve, turn the mousse out on to a plate and add bunches of watercress. If you are taking the mousse on a picnic, then pack it in a mould which has a tight-fitting lid. Keep it on ice until ready to serve it, then turn out and garnish.

Beetroot Roulade

Serves 6

This is light and delicate, and perfect for a warm sunny day. Serve with a large green salad.

175 g/6 oz Emmental cheese
50 g/2 oz fresh breadcrumbs
salt and pepper
100 g/4 oz cooked beetroot
150 ml/¼ pint soured cream
4 eggs, separated
handful of fine dry white breadcrumbs
FILLING
225 g/8 oz Ricotta cheese
4 tablespoons creamed horseradish

Grate the cheese and mix it with the breadcrumbs, then stir in seasoning. Grate the beetroot, add it to the mixture and stir in the soured cream with the egg yolks.

Line a 23 × 33 cm/9 × 13 in Swiss roll tin with greaseproof paper. Grease this thoroughly and sprinkle the base with the dry breadcrumbs. Whisk the egg whites until they stand in stiff peaks, fold into the beetroot mixture and turn it into the tin. Pour it evenly over the surface, then spread out gently, trying not to disturb the crumbs.

Bake the roulade in a moderately hot oven (200c, 400f, gas 6) for 10 to 12 minutes, until set. While the roulade is cooking beat the cheese and creamed horseradish together. Turn the roulade out on to a clean sheet of greaseproof paper and remove the cooking paper. Allow to cool. Spread the filling over and roll up, using the greaseproof paper as a guide.

Trim off the ends, sprinkle with grated raw beetroot and serve sliced.

Note: If the cheese mixture seems too thick, add a little cream.

Stuffed Potato Shells
Serves 6

6 large potatoes
melted butter for brushing
COTTAGE CHEESE FILLING
3 sticks celery
2 large dessert apples
a few spring onions
100 g/4 oz walnuts or salted peanuts
handful of sultanas
freshly grated nutmeg
salt and pepper
350 g/12 oz cottage cheese
CARROT AND RADISH FILLING
225 g/8 oz carrots, grated
juice of 1 lemon
bunch of radishes, thinly sliced
2 tablespoons chopped chives
100 g/4 oz wholemeal breadcrumbs
50 g/2 oz butter
4 tablespoons soured cream
MUSHROOM AND COURGETTE FILLING
225 g/8 oz button mushrooms, sliced
2 courgettes, finely sliced
1 red onion, chopped
2 tablespoons chopped fresh marjoram
150 ml/¼ pint soured cream

Bake the potatoes in their jackets in a moderately hot oven (200c, 400f, gas 6) for about an hour or until they are cooked through. Leave them to cool slightly, then cut each one in half and scoop out the middle using a small spoon. Leave a fairly thick skin, then brush the potato shells with melted butter, both inside and out, and place them on a baking tray. Put them back in the oven for a further 20 minutes, or until the shells are really crisp.

For the cottage cheese filling, chop the celery, core and chop the apples and the spring onions. Mix all these ingredients with the walnuts or peanuts, sultanas, a good sprinkling of nutmeg and seasoning, and the cottage cheese.

For the second filling, mix the carrots, lemon juice, radishes and chives and put them in a bowl. Fry the breadcrumbs in the butter until crisp, then turn into the bowl and mix with the cream. Mix all the ingredients for the mushroom and courgette filling.

When the potato skins are cooked, fill them with the mixtures and serve as soon as possible. If you like, leave the skins to cool before filling them but do not fill them too long before you eat them or they will become soggy and dreary.

Filled Cottage Loaf
Serves 6 to 8

1 cottage loaf
75 g/3 oz butter
EGG AND WATERCRESS FILLING
knob of butter
3 eggs, lightly beaten
bunch of watercress, chopped
2 tablespoons mayonnaise
salt and pepper
TUNA FILLING
1 (198 g/7 oz) can tuna in oil
225 g/8 oz cottage cheese
25 g/1 oz stuffed green olives, sliced
dash of Tabasco sauce
SWEET CORN FILLING
½ cup alfalfa sprouts or bean sprouts
100 g/4 oz frozen sweet corn, defrosted
6 radishes, thinly sliced
4 tablespoons mayonnaise

Slice the top-knot off the loaf then cut the base into three even layers. Butter.

For the egg and watercress filling melt the butter in a small non-stick saucepan. Add the eggs and cook over a low heat, stirring continuously, until scrambled.

Remove from the heat and cool completely, stir in the chopped watercress, mayonnaise and seasoning. Chill while preparing the other fillings.

For the second filling drain and flake the tuna, then combine with the cottage cheese and olives. Season to taste with Tabasco, salt and pepper, being careful not to add too much Tabasco as it is very hot. Finally make the sweet corn filling by combining all the ingredients and season well.

Sandwich the loaf together with the three fillings. The whole loaf can then be cut into wedges and put back together. Wrap securely in cling film.

Filled Lychees

Serves 4   *To serve with drinks.*

20 canned lychees
50 g/2 oz peanuts, roasted and finely chopped
a little finely chopped fresh root ginger (about
1 teaspoon is enough or the filling will be
too hot)
50 g/2 oz Philadelphia cheese

This is very fiddly — I warn you!

Thoroughly drain and dry the lychees. Beat the nuts and ginger into the cheese, then use a small spoon to press this mixture into the stoned lychees. Chill before serving.

Note: If you possess a cherry stoner, stone some cherries and stuff with this mixture.

Stuffed Pitta Breads

Serves 8   *Stuffed pittas make ideal picnic food because they travel well*

RICE FILLING
100 g/4 oz brown or white rice
4 tablespoons well-seasoned vinaigrette
100 g/4 oz mozzarella cheese
7.5 cm/3 in piece cucumber
4 tomatoes

a few basil leaves, chopped
salt and pepper
4 pitta breads
ALFALFA FILLING
1 (100 g/4 oz) packet mixed salted nuts
100 g/4 oz alfalfa sprouts
1 dessert apple, cored and chopped
175 g/6 oz smoked applewood cheese, diced (or your favourite cheese)
4 tablespoons natural yogurt
4 wholewheat pittas

Cook the rice in boiling water until just tender. Drain then stir in the vinaigrette while the rice is still hot. As the mixture cools the rice will absorb the dressing which gives it a good flavour.

Meanwhile slice the cheese, cucumber and tomatoes quite small. When the rice is cold, stir together with the basil and seasoning. Split the pittas along one long edge and carefully open up the pockets. Divide the filling between the pittas, then wrap securely in cling film.

For the second filling, roughly chop the nuts and stir into the sprouts with the apple, cheese and yogurt; season well. Split the pittas down one long side and open up the pockets carefully, then using a spoon divide the filling between them. Wrap individually in cling film.

Out-In-The-Country Pie

Serves 6

This tasty pie is easy to cut into slices and it won't lose all its filling en route.

225 g/8 oz plain flour
225 g/8 oz wholemeal flour
salt and pepper
bunch of mixed herbs, including some thyme, a few sprigs of sage and plenty of parsley
225 g/8 oz butter or margarine
about 6 tablespoons cold water

FILLING

225 g/8 oz cooked chicken
100 g/4 oz cooked ham
bunch of spring onions, chopped
225 g/8 oz cottage cheese
freshly grated nutmeg
2 (227 g/8 oz) packets frozen spinach
50 g/2 oz butter, melted
2 eggs, beaten
2 tablespoons double cream
beaten egg to glaze

Mix both types of flour in a bowl, then add a pinch of salt. Chop the herbs. Cut the butter or margarine into pieces and rub it into the flour, then add the herbs and mix well. Stir in enough water to bind the pastry, wrap and chill for a while, then turn out on to a floured surface and knead lightly. Cut about two-thirds off the pastry and set the rest aside. Roll the dough into a circle large enough to line a fairly deep 25 cm/10 in round loose-bottomed flan tin. Press the pastry into the tin, leaving all the excess at the edges. Chill until the filling is ready.

Mince or finely chop the chicken and ham, and put in a bowl. Add the onions, cottage cheese, plenty of seasoning and a generous amount of nutmeg. Cook the spinach according to the packet instruction and drain thoroughly. Stir in the melted butter, then add the spinach to the chicken mixture. Beat the eggs and cream together and mix everything together. Put this mixture into the pastry case, pressing it down well.

Roll out the reserved pastry into a circle large enough to cover the top of the pie. Lift the pastry on top of the filling, trimming off excess. Brush the very edge of the pastry top with beaten egg, then fold down the edge of the pastry sides to seal the filling in completely. Press the pastry join with a fork to seal it well and make it look attractive. Brush with a little beaten egg and make a small hole in the middle to allow steam to escape.

Bake the pie in a moderately hot oven (200c, 400f, gas 6) for 20 minutes, then reduce the oven temperature to moderate (180c, 350f, gas 4) and cook for a further 20 minutes. Remove from the oven and leave to cool. While the pie is still warm, loosen it from the sides of the tin by gently lifting the base, then leave to cool completely.

An easy way to remove flans and pies from loose-bottomed tins is to stand the tin on a storage jar, then ease the side down. When cold cut into slices and put back in the shape of the pie, then wrap in cling film for taking on the picnic. It can be made a day or two in advance and stored in the refrigerator.

Portable Instant Picnics

Cut oranges into wedges, then pack them tightly in cling film and chill. Cucumber, melons, grapefruit or pineapple can also be cut into pieces, re-shaped and packed in this way. Put the packages in bags of ice to keep really cool.

Green Bean Salad
Serves 4

450 g/1 lb young French beans, trimmed

75 g/3 oz pine nuts, lightly toasted

6 slices bread

50 g/2 oz butter

2 tablespoons olive oil

1 clove garlic, crushed

4 eggs, hard-boiled

1 red onion, thinly sliced

1 tablespoon chopped fresh marjoram

DRESSING

4 tablespoons olive oil

2 tablespoons cider vinegar

1 tablespoon clear honey

salt and pepper

2 teaspoons wholegrain mustard

Steam the beans for 3 to 5 minutes, so that they are tender but still very crisp. Put the beans in a bowl with the pine nuts.

Cut the crusts off the bread if you like, then cut the slices into small cubes. Melt the butter with the oil in a large pan. When hot add the garlic and the bread cubes. Cook, stirring and turning the cubes frequently, until they are evenly brown and crisp. Discard garlic. Drain on absorbent kitchen paper and add these croûtons to the beans and pine nuts.

Quarter the eggs and separate the onion slices into rings, then add both to the salad. If you are taking this a distance, pack it into a container at this point and take the dressing separately, to be added at the last minute. Sprinkle the marjoram over the top. Put all the dressing ingredients together in a screw-topped jar and shake well, then pour this over the salad. Lightly toss.

Asparagus with Ham Sauce
Serves 4

450 g / 1 lb asparagus spears, trimmed
salt and pepper
100 g / 4 oz cooked ham, minced
1 tablespoon Dijon mustard
150 ml / ¼ pint soured cream
2 tablespoons lemon juice

Tie the asparagus in a neat bundle, then cook it in boiling salted water for about 7 to 10 minutes. Drain and set aside. Mix all the sauce ingredients and chill. Serve with the asparagus.

Strawberry Coeur à la Crème

Take a basket of strawberries to serve with traditional coeur à la crème. Make the coeur à la crème by beating a little cream taken from 150 ml / ¼ pint double cream into 225 g / 8 oz cream cheese. Whip the remaining cream with a couple of tablespoons of icing sugar, then fold it into the cream cheese. Whisk an egg white until stiff and fold in. Spoon the mixture into muslin-lined coeur à la crème moulds and stand them on a plate or dish in the refrigerator. Leave overnight, then pack the drained coeur à la crème moulds in cling film and put in a chiller box. Turn them out on the picnic and have with the strawberries.

Gooseberry Flan

Serves 6 to 8

150 g/5 oz wholemeal flour

150 g/5 oz plain flour

175 g/6 oz butter

75 g/3 oz toasted hazelnuts, ground

2 tablespoons demerara sugar

about 3 tablespoons water

GINGER CREAM FILLING

25 g/1 oz cornflour

15 g/½ oz caster sugar

300 ml/½ pint milk

1 vanilla pod, split

2 egg yolks

2 pieces preserved stem ginger, chopped

2 tablespoons ginger syrup (from the preserved ginger)

1 egg white

GOOSEBERRY FILLING

1 kg/2 lb gooseberries

100 g/4 oz sugar

150 ml/¼ pint water

15 g/½ oz gelatine

Mix the flours in a bowl, rub in the butter then add the nuts and sugar. Stir in just enough water to bind the ingredients and mix them together to form a dough. Roll out the pastry and use to line an oblong tin measuring about 8½ × 12 in/21 × 30 cm. Prick the base all over with a fork and lay a piece of greaseproof paper on top. Sprinkle in dried peas or beans and bake the pastry case in a moderately hot oven (200c, 400F, gas 6) for 10 minutes. Remove the greaseproof paper and peas or beans then bake for a further 5 to 10 minutes or until brown and crisp. Leave to cool.

To make the ginger cream filling, mix the cornflour and caster sugar to a smooth paste with a little of the milk. Bring the remaining milk to the boil with the vanilla pod, leave to infuse for 10 minutes, then strain the milk on to the cornflour mixture. Pour the mixture back into the saucepan and bring to the boil, stirring all the time. Cook for 2 minutes then remove from the heat and beat in the egg yolks, ginger and syrup. Leave until cool.

Top and tail the gooseberries. Dissolve the sugar in the water, then poach the fruit in this syrup for 1 to 2 minutes until just softened but still whole. Soften the gelatine in a little cold water. Off the heat, add the gelatine to the gooseberries and stir until it dissolves. Cool.

To finish the ginger cream, whisk the egg white until stiff and fold it into the cream. Spread this in the pastry case, then top with the gooseberries. Chill until completely set. Wrap securely in a double thickness of foil.

Apple cake
Serves 10

450 g / 1 lb cooking apples
450 g / 1 lb self-raising flour
3 teaspoons baking powder
½ teaspoon ground cinnamon
50 g / 2 oz walnuts
grated rind of 1 orange
grated rind of 1 lemon
225 g / 8 oz caster sugar
100 ml / 4 fl oz sunflower oil
3 eggs

You could fold in a handful of blueberries as well as the apple.

Peel and core the apples, then cut into chunks. Sift the flour with the baking powder and cinnamon. Chop the walnuts with the apples in a food processor until finely chopped but not slushy. Add the orange and lemon rind.

Beat the sugar, oil and eggs together until light and fluffy. Fold in the dry ingredients, then fold in the apple and nut mixture. Turn into a greased 25 cm / 10 in springform tin and bake in a moderate oven (180C, 350F, gas 4) for 1¾ hours or until a skewer inserted into the cake comes out clean. Turn out and cool the cake on a wire rack.

Cashew and coriander shortbread
Makes 24

100 g/4 oz butter
50 g/2 oz caster sugar
150 g/5 oz plain flour
25 g/1 oz rice flour
100 g/4 oz cashew nuts, ground
coarsely grated rind of 2 large oranges
3 teaspoons ground coriander

Cream the butter with the sugar until very soft and pale, then mix in the flour, rice flour, cashew nuts, orange rind and coriander. Press the mixture into a greased 20 cm/8 in square tin and bake in a moderate oven (180c, 350F, gas 4) for 1 hour.

Cut the shortbread into pieces and leave them in the tin for 5 minutes before carefully lifting them on to a wire rack to cool.

Sunday biscuits
Makes about 20

These can be made in a flash – useful when the sun is shining and you feel lazy.

100 g/4 oz butter, softened
100 g/4 oz demerara sugar
100 g/4 oz flaked coconut
100 g/4 oz ground rice
50 g/2 oz cornflour
about 4 tablespoons milk

Mix all the ingredients together, adding enough milk to make a soft consistency. Put little mounds of the mixture well apart on greased baking trays and bake in a moderate oven (180c, 350F, gas 4) for about 15 minutes or until brown and crisp. Leave to cool slightly on the tins, then transfer to wire racks to cool completely.

Sandwiches

You don't need a recipe as such for sandwiches, do you? Of course not. So these are really just a few filling ideas to give you a starting point. Sandwiches are, or should be, spur of the moment things, made with whatever takes your fancy at the time.

- Grated carrot, raisins and mayonnaise
- Smoked chicken with finely chopped watercress
- Smoked salmon with shredded spring onion and capers
- Flaked mackerel and chopped hard boiled egg
- Thin shredded ham with sliced apple and chutney
- Peanut butter with sliced pear
- Sprouting beans with chopped turkey and mayonnaise
- Alfalfa with cream cheese and prosciutto
- Smoked trout well mixed with creamed
- horseradish
- Mozzarella and tomato
- etc., etc., etc.

Home-made mayonnaise

Home-made mayonnaise is by far the best. Whisk 2 egg yolks with a pinch of dry mustard and seasoning. Add a little lemon juice and a few drops of oil and whisk thoroughly until well combined. Whisking all the time, gradually add 250 ml/8fl oz oil, pouring it in drop by drop. When the mixture is very creamy add lemon juice to taste. Chill lightly.

Basic home-made lemonade
Serves 8

pared rind and juice of 6 lemons
1.15 litres/2 pints water
honey to taste
· several sprigs of lemon balm

Put the lemon rind and juice in a saucepan and pour
in the water. Add some honey, bring to the boil, then
remove from the heat and add the herb sprigs. Leave
to cool slightly before adding more honey to taste. Stir,
then leave to cool completely. Strain and chill.
Note: If you like, pulverise chopped lemons with sugar,
pour boiling water over them and leave until cold.
Pour through a sieve.

Tomato cooler
Serves 4

900 ml / 1 ½ pints tomato juice
juice of ½ lemon
a little grated lemon rind
generous dash of Tabasco sauce
generous dash of Worcestershire sauce
plenty of ice
a few sprigs of mint

Mix all the ingredients and pour into a vacuum flask
to carry on the picnic. Alternatively, thoroughly chill
the drink, pour it into a bottle and put this in a chiller
box to keep cool.

Sparkling fruit juice

For a cool, long drink mix peach juice or passion
fruit juice with sparkling white wine or champagne.
Pour the fruit juice into tall glasses and add plenty
of crushed ice. Try using some of the unusual fruit
juices you can now buy — pear, guava, plum, mango
and grape are some that taste delicious mixed in
this way.

Summer milk shakes

People often forget how delicious fresh fruit milk
shakes are. Children love them. Blend chilled milk
with enough honey to sweeten and whatever fruit
happens to be available.

To Have With Drinks

We have become a nation of wine drinkers, and that has simplified what to give to people who don't care for spirits.

If you are having friends in just for drinks, then it's nice to offer something to eat with them but if the people are staying to dinner, then make the offering non-filling: just something to set their tastebuds going. Otherwise (as we often say to children) they won't be able to eat their dinner up. Always try and have some prepared raw vegetables for the dieters and for those who know there is something delicious to come.

Stilton Savouries

Makes
about 30

100 g/4 oz plain flour	
100 g/4 oz unsalted butter, chilled and cubed	
100 g/4 oz Stilton cheese, crumbled	
beaten egg to glaze	
75 g/3 oz walnuts, chopped	

Put the flour, butter and Stilton in a food processor and mix briefly to give a smooth dough. Alternatively, knead all the ingredients together by hand. Wrap and chill for 1 hour or until firm.

Roll out the dough to 5 cm/¼ in thick. Cut into 5 cm/2 in squares, then cut the squares in half diagonally to make triangles. Place on several greased baking sheets and chill for 10 minutes. Brush with beaten egg and sprinkle with chopped walnuts. Bake in a moderately hot oven (190c, 375f, gas 5) for 5 to 7 minutes, or until golden. Transfer to a wire rack to cool. These nibbles can be served hot or warm, or they can be made in advance and briefly reheated before serving or they can be frozen.

Small Vegetable Tarts

Makes 12

Select the freshest, best quality vegetables for these tarts – you won't need large quantities but have a good mixture. Flavour the mayonnaise with lots of chopped herbs, if you like.

50 g/2 oz butter, softened	
100 g/4 oz cream cheese	
100 g/4 oz self-raising flour	
salt and pepper	
thinly sliced carrot, tiny cauliflower florets, thinly sliced courgettes, short lengths of French bean	
150 ml/¼ pint mayonnaise	
1–2 cloves garlic, crushed (optional)	

Beat the butter with the cream cheese, then gradually work in the flour and a pinch of salt to make a soft dough. On a lightly floured surface, gently knead the dough into a ball and roll it out thinly. Cut out 12 circles to line patty tins. Press the pastry into the tins, prick all over and chill for 30 minutes.

For the filling the vegetables should be barely cooked. They are best cooked separately by steaming and 3 to 5 minutes is quite long enough. Leave them to cool.

Bake the tartlet cases in a moderately hot oven (200c, 400f, gas 6) for 10 to 15 minutes or until the pastry is crisp and golden. Leave the tarts in the tins for a few minutes, then transfer them to a wire rack to cool.

Pile the vegetables (separately or mixed) in the pastry cases. Season the mayonnaise and mix it with the garlic (if you like), then top each of the tarts with some mayonnaise.

Asparagus tips, broccoli, tiny peas cooked with shredded lettuce or baby broad beans.

Other Vegetables to Try

Crispy Potato Skins

Brush a baking tin with sunflower oil, then add thin strips of scrubbed and dried potato peelings and sprinkle a little oil over them. Arrange the pieces of skin in one layer and sprinkle with coarse sea salt. Bake in a moderately hot oven (190c, 375f, gas 5), turning once or twice, for about 20 minutes, until brown and crisp.

These go particularly well with a dip.

Or bake potatoes in the usual way — scoop out the potato (use for mash) spread the skins with a little butter or margarine and a strip of cheese. Bake till bubbling.

Special Egg Tarts
Makes 12

12 small pastry tart shells	
FILLING	
3 eggs	
6 tablespoons single cream	
salt and pepper	
50 g/2 oz butter	
bunch of chives, chopped	
100 g/4 oz smoked salmon pieces, chopped	

Make the tart shells according to the recipe instructions.

Beat the eggs with the cream and seasoning. Melt the butter in a small, non-stick saucepan over a fairly low heat. Pour in the eggs and cook, stirring all the time, until they set. Do not overcook them or they will curdle.

Remove the pan from the heat and stir in the chives and the smoked salmon. Put spoonfuls of the mixture into the tart shells and serve warm or cold.

Note: Serve as a first course or with drinks.

Guacomole
Serves 4

| 2 ripe avocados |
| 1 tomato, peeled and chopped |
| 1 tablespoon chopped spring onion |
| juice of a clove of garlic |
| 1 tablespoon lemon juice |
| salt and pepper |
| fresh coriander leaves |

Peel and chop the avocados. Place in a liquidiser or food processor with the other ingredients and whizz until well mixed. Serve with tortilla chips.

Note: Don't leave Guacomole too long because it discolours. It helps if you push the avocado stone into the centre and cover with cling film, but it's still nicer if it isn't left too long.

Cheese Nut Ball with Fruit
Serves 12

| 50 g/2 oz Cheddar cheese, grated |
| 100 g/4 oz Stilton cheese, crumbled |
| 450 g/1 lb cream cheese |
| 2 tablespoons soured cream |
| 2 teaspoons red wine |
| 1 tablespoon chopped parsley |
| 275 g/10 oz mixed nuts, chopped (try walnuts or cashews) |

Blend the cheeses together with the soured cream and red wine. Stir in the chopped parsley, then chill until firm.

Sprinkle the nuts on to a wooden board, or clean surface, and turn out the cheese mixture on top. Carefully roll the cheese into a ball, coating it evenly in the nuts.

Chill the cheese ball for at least 30 minutes, or until required, then serve with sliced apples, celery and crackers.

Note: Odds and ends of cheese, leftover from a cheeseboard, can be used in this cheese ball.

Filled Chicory Leaves
Serves 6 to 8

2 (200 g/7 oz) cans tuna in oil
4 gherkins, chopped
1 tablespoon capers
½ teaspoon ground coriander
a few spring onions, chopped
1 generous tablespoon bean sprouts
salt and pepper
enough mayonnaise to bind together
2 heads chicory

You can fill celery with the same mixture

Drain and flake the tuna, then add the gherkins, capers, coriander, spring onions and bean sprouts. Sprinkle in seasoning to taste and stir in the mayonnaise.

Separate the chicory leaves and pile a little of the tuna mixture on each leaf. Arrange the stuffed chicory leaves in a fan-shape.

Note: Try filling radicchio leaves or tiny lettuce leaves instead of the chicory leaves.

Brie in Pastry
Makes
up to 30

450 g/1 lb prepared filo dough
50 g/2 oz butter, melted
225 g/8 oz firm Brie, thoroughly chilled
beaten egg to glaze

Keep any extra sheets of filo pastry covered in cling film as you work. Cut the pastry into 5 cm/2 in wide strips, measuring about 15 cm/6 in in length. Brush them with melted butter. Cut the cheese into 1 cm/½ in dice and place one piece at one end of each strip of pastry. Fold the pastry over and over to enclose the cheese in a triangle shape completely, and tuck the end in neatly.

Place on greased baking trays and chill for 15 minutes. Brush the pastry with beaten egg and bake in a hot oven (220C, 425F, gas 7) for 5 to 7 minutes, until puffed and golden. Serve warm.

Note: A quick alternative is to prepare a whole, small Camembert in pastry. Scrape off the rind, then chill the cheese very thoroughly in a freezer: it should be almost frozen before it is wrapped and baked as above.

Spinach Balls
Makes 40

100 g/4 oz frozen chopped spinach, thawed
50 g/2 oz Parmesan cheese, grated
50 g/2 oz butter
150 ml/¼ pint milk and water (half and half, mixed)
75 g/3 oz plain flour
pinch of salt
2 eggs, beaten

Thoroughly drain the spinach and purée it with the cheese. Place the butter and liquid in a saucepan and heat slowly until the butter melts. Stir in the spinach purée, bring rapidly to the boil, then immediately stir in all the flour and salt. Stir quickly so that the mixture forms a smooth ball of paste which leaves the sides of the pan clean. Allow to cool slightly, then beat in the eggs until smooth and glossy.

Drop tiny, neat spoonfuls of the mixture on to greased baking trays and bake in a moderately hot oven (200C, 400F, gas 6) for 15 to 20 minutes until puffed and golden. Leave to cool on a wire rack.

Cheese and Parsley Biscuits

These are so good eaten with apples and cheese.

Makes 12

100 g/4 oz wholemeal flour
50 g/2 oz medium oatmeal
pinch of salt
75 g/3 oz sunflower margarine
75 g/3 oz cheese, grated
bunch of parsley, chopped

Mix the flour with the oatmeal and a generous pinch of salt. Add the margarine, cut it into pieces then rub it into the dry ingredients. Stir in the cheese and parsley. Knead the mixture together to form a dough. Alternatively, mix all the ingredients in a food processor.

Roll out on a lightly floured surface and cut out 12 biscuits. Place on greased baking trays and bake in a moderate oven (180C, 350F, gas 4) for 20 to 25 minutes or until golden.

Leave the biscuits on the trays for a few minutes, then transfer them to a wire rack to cool completely.

Sesame Crackers

Makes about 16

225 g/8 oz wholewheat semolina
100 g/4 oz wholemeal flour
1 teaspoon ground coriander
1 teaspoon grated nutmeg
100 g/4 oz butter
50 g/2 oz sesame seeds
1 egg, beaten
about 50 ml/2 fl oz water
1 tablespoon coarse sea salt
extra sesame seeds to sprinkle over the crackers

Mix the semolina with the flour and spices in a bowl. Rub in the butter until the mixture is like fine breadcrumbs, then stir in the sesame seeds. Add the egg and about half the water, mix in the dry ingredients to make a stiff dough, adding more water as needed.

Turn the dough out on to a floured surface and knead it gently, then roll it out into a large thin 25 cm/10 in square. Cut the dough into about 16 squares — more if you want to make the crackers smaller — then press the crackers on greased baking trays to make them thin and sprinkle with coarse salt and sesame seeds. Press the salt lightly into the dough and bake the crackers in a moderate oven (180c, 350f, gas 4) for about 8 to 10 minutes. Leave on the trays briefly, then transfer to a wire rack to cool completely.

Popcorn with Nuts

65 g/2½ oz butter
150 g/5 oz popping corn
25 g/1 oz hazelnuts
25 g/1 oz brazil nuts
25 g/1 oz almonds
25 g/1 oz walnuts
CARAMEL
425 g/15 oz butter
275 g/10 oz sugar

For this you will need a large saucepan with a tight-fitting lid. Melt the butter in the saucepan and heat it until a haze can be seen above the fat. Add the popcorn, immediately reduce the heat to low and put the lid on the pan. Shake the pan vigorously until all the popping has ceased. Remove from the heat and add the nuts.

In another pan, mix the butter and sugar for the caramel until the sugar has dissolved, then simmer until the mixture turns golden. Pour the caramel over the popcorn and nut mixture and stir well.

Variation **Savoury Popcorn** Make a batch of popcorn (cook the corn in hot sunflower oil in a large covered saucepan) and turn it into a large bowl. Sprinkle with salt and offer the corn with drinks.

Children's Honey Snack

This is fun for children when you have friends in for drinks. Give the children a glass of sparkling spring water with a slice of lemon and a bowlful of this to keep them happy.

75 g/3 oz desiccated coconut
75 g/3 oz jumbo oats
75 g/3 oz crunchy breakfast cereal
150 g/5 oz mixed nuts
3 tablespoons sunflower oil
1 tablespoon brown sugar
2–3 tablespoons honey

Mix all the ingredients together and spread the mixture out on a baking tray. Bake in a moderate oven (180c, 350f, gas 4) for about 30 minutes, or until the snack is crisp and brown. Turn the mixture occasionally during cooking and again at the end of the cooking time. Allow to cool on the tin before storing in an airtight container.

Jeannie's Pickled Cucumbers with Ham

Roll each large pickled cucumber in cream cheese, then wrap in very thinly sliced ham. Cover and leave in the fridge for an hour or so, then cut into slices.

Let Them Eat Cake

Tea parties have rather fallen out of fashion. Now, if someone invites you for tea, it's more likely to be just a cup of tea in the kitchen and a forage around in the biscuit tin. Where are those teas you read about in novels – thin cucumber sandwiches and strawberries and cream on a hot summer day, or toasted crumpets on a chilly winter afternoon in front of a log fire with delicious slices of fruit-filled cake? Ah, well . . . here are some of my family teatime favourites.

Simple Weekend Cake

Makes a
20 cm/8 in
cake

This is quick to make and useful if you suddenly find you have extra guests.

275 g/10 oz plain flour
½ teaspoon salt
½ teaspoon bicarbonate of soda
2 teaspoons baking powder
175 g/6 oz light soft brown sugar
grated rind of 1 orange
50 g/2 oz walnuts, chopped
2 ripe bananas, mashed
175 g/6 oz carrots, grated
3 eggs, beaten
175 ml/6 fl oz sunflower oil
SIMPLE FROSTING
175 g/6 oz Philadelphia cream cheese
2 generous tablespoons frozen concentrated orange juice
2 tablespoons icing sugar
about 6 tablespoons crème fraîche

Sift the flour, salt, bicarbonate of soda and baking powder into a bowl. Add the sugar, orange rind, walnuts, bananas and carrots. Mix well, then add the eggs and the sunflower oil and beat for 1 minute.

Line the base of a 20 cm/8 in deep cake tin with greaseproof paper and grease the tin. Turn the mixture into the tin and bake in a moderate oven (180c, 350f, gas 4) for 1 hour 20 minutes or until a skewer inserted into the cake comes out clean. Turn the cake out to cool on a wire rack.

Put the cream cheese into a bowl, then beat in the remaining ingredients for the frosting. Pile this on top of the cooled cake, or slit the cake horizontally and sandwich it together with frosting if you prefer.

Fresh Peach Cake

This is one of those useful recipes because you can freeze the cake on a day when you are not very busy and it's delicious to have either with tea or as a dessert.

Makes a
23 cm/9 in
cake

4 eggs
100 g/4 oz caster sugar
grated rind of 2 lemons
100 g/4 oz plain flour
25 g/1 oz butter, melted
FILLING
6 ripe peaches
300 ml/½ pint double cream
4 tablespoons rum
2 tablespoons icing sugar
8 ratafia biscuits

Beat the eggs and sugar together with the lemon rind until they are very pale and thick. Sift the flour and gently fold it into the eggs. Lastly fold in the melted butter.

Line the base of two 23 cm/9 in sandwich tins with greaseproof paper and grease them thoroughly. Divide the mixture between the tins and bake the cakes in a moderately hot oven (190c, 375f, gas 5) for about 25 minutes or until a skewer inserted into the cake comes out clean. Remove the cakes from their tins and leave them to cool on a wire rack.

Put the peaches in a large bowl and pour on enough boiling water to cover them. Leave for a minute, then drain and peel the fruit. Halve the peaches, remove the stones and chop. Put the cream, rum and icing sugar in a bowl, then whip the mixture until firm. Crumble the ratafias and mix them with the chopped peaches. When they are well combined, fold the mixture into the whipped cream.

Sandwich the two sponges together with about two-thirds of the mixture, then spread the rest over the top. Chill well before serving.

Poppy Seed Pound Cake

Makes an
18 cm/7 in
cake

225 g/8 oz butter
225 g/8 oz caster sugar
grated rind of 1 lemon
4 eggs
225 g/8 oz self-raising flour
½ teaspoon ground cinnamon
100 g/4 oz poppy seeds
2 tablespoons milk

Cream the butter with the sugar and lemon rind until soft and pale. Add the eggs, then add the flour and cinnamon, then the poppy seeds, gently folding everything in. Lastly add the milk.

Line and grease an 18 cm/7 in deep round cake tin. Turn the mixture into the tin and bake in a moderate oven (160c, 325F, gas 3) for 1½ hours or until a skewer inserted into the cake comes out clean. Check the cake towards the end of the cooking time and if it looks very brown on top cover with a piece of cooking foil.

Turn the cake out on to a wire rack to cool. Sprinkle the top with a little caster sugar while still hot.

Lumpy Buns

Makes 14

These are as easy to make as old-fashioned rock cakes but they taste much nicer.

225 g/8 oz Granary flour
2 teaspoons baking powder
100 g/4 oz butter, cut into small pieces
handful of cracked wheat
50 g/2 oz rye flakes
75 g/3 oz currants
grated rind of 1 orange
2 tablespoons chopped crystallised fruit
25 g/1 oz desiccated coconut
50 g/2 oz demerara sugar
1 teaspoon ground mixed spice
2 eggs, beaten

Put the flour and baking powder in a bowl, then add the butter and rub it in. Alternatively, put the ingredients in a food processor and process until fine. Stir in the cracked wheat, rye flakes and currants. Add the orange rind, crystallised fruit, coconut, sugar and spice, then mix really well. Stir in the eggs to make a fairly firm mixture.

Take spoonfuls of the mixture (there is enough to make 14 buns) and place them slightly apart on greased baking trays. Bake in a moderately hot oven (200C, 400F, gas 6) for 15 minutes or until risen and golden. Cool on wire racks.

Note: You can bake these in greased muffin pans.

Peach and Almond Cake

Demerara sugar and chopped toasted almonds give this cake a wonderfully crunchy crust.

Serves 12

175 g/6 oz butter or margarine
175 g/6 oz caster sugar
grated rind of 1 orange
3 eggs
175 g/6 oz self-raising flour
100 g/4 oz ground almonds
100 g/4 oz dried peaches (some may need soaking), chopped (or use ordinary dried apricots, soaked overnight and thoroughly drained)
150 g/5 oz blanched almonds, chopped
2 tablespoons orange juice
2 tablespoons demerara sugar

Cream the butter or margarine with the sugar and orange rind until pale and very soft, then beat in the eggs. Mix the flour, ground almonds, peach and most of the chopped nuts (save a small handful for the top of the cake), then fold these ingredients into the cake. Add the orange juice, stirring very gently, to soften the mixture.

Line a 20 cm/8 in round deep cake tin with

greaseproof paper and grease the tin. Turn the mixture into the tin, then sprinkle the demerara sugar and remaining nuts on top. Bake in a moderate oven (160C, 325F, gas 3) for 1½ hours. Turn the cake out on to a wire rack to cool.

Sinful Chocolate Cake

Makes a
23 cm/9 in
cake

If I had to choose one cake this would be it!

225 g/8 oz butter
225 g/8 oz caster sugar
6 eggs, separated
225 g/8 oz plain chocolate, melted
150 g/5 oz ground almonds
150 g/5 oz plain flour

Beat the butter and sugar together until pale and creamy, then add the egg yolks and beat well. Slowly add the melted chocolate and mix thoroughly. Using a metal spoon, fold in the ground almonds and flour.

In a separate bowl, whisk the egg whites until they are stiff, then fold these into the cake mixture. If this is difficult, stir a little of the white in first to soften the mixture. Pour into a well-greased 23 cm/9 in springform tin and bake in a moderate oven (180C, 350F, gas 4) for 60 to 70 minutes or until firm. Leave to cool in the tin before turning out.

Note: This cake also makes a great pudding, served with whipped cream, can you bear the guilt?

Apricot Cookies

Makes
about 26

100 g/4 oz butter or margarine
100 g/4 oz granulated sugar
50 g/2 oz light brown sugar
1 egg
1 teaspoon vanilla essence
150 g/5 oz plain flour
½ teaspoon salt
½ teaspoon bicarbonate of soda
175 g/6 oz dried apricots, coarsely chopped

Cream together the butter, s[...]
essence until smooth. Gradual[...]
salt and bicarbonate of soda and [...]
the apricots and stir well.

Put teaspoonfuls of the mixtur[...]
apart on greased baking trays and ba[...]
hot oven (190C, 375F, gas 5) for 10 [...]
the cookies are evenly golden. Allow t[...]
the baking trays before transferring to [...]

*These are [...]
particularly [...]
nice with [...]
choc[...]*

Kate H[...] Brownies
Makes 16

100 g/4 oz butter	
50 g/2 oz plain chocolate	
225 g/8 oz sugar	
¼ teaspoon vanilla essence	
75 g/3 oz self-raising flour	
2 eggs	
100 g/4 oz chopped walnuts	

Melt the butter and chocolate in a heavy-based saucepan over a very low heat, stirring continuously. Stir
in the sugar and vanilla, then remove the pan from
the heat and stir in the flour. Beat in the eggs, one
at a time, and stir in the walnuts.

Line a 20 cm/8 in square cake tin with greaseproof
paper and grease the tin. Pour in the mixture and
bake in a moderate oven (160C, 325F, gas 3) for 50
to 60 minutes or until the edges begin to shrink from
the sides of the tin. Cool in the tin before cutting into
squares.

*It is very typical
of Kate that
if she decides
to do something
she does it
better than most.
As a chocolate
lover she has
only the best
chocolate
recipes. She
makes these
chocolate
brownies and
naturally they
are the best.*

Ginger Thins
Makes
about 30

225 g/8 oz plain flour
2 teaspoons ground ginger
100 g/4 oz butter, diced
175 g/6 oz light soft brown sugar
1 egg, beaten

Grease several baking trays. Sift the flour and ginger
into a mixing bowl. Add the butter and rub it in until

...ture resembles fine breadcrumbs. Stir in the
...ar and enough of the beaten egg to make a stiff
...dough. Turn on to a floured surface and knead quickly
until smooth. Shape into a 2.5 cm/1 in diameter roll.

Wrap in cooking foil or cling film and place in the
deep freeze until almost frozen. Using a very sharp
knife, cut the mixture into thin slices. Place well apart
on the prepared baking trays and bake in a moderately
hot oven (190C, 375F, gas 5) for 5 to 7 minutes, or
until golden. Cool the thins on the baking trays for a
few minutes, then transfer them to a wire rack to cool
completely.

Old Fashioned Butter Cookies
Makes 20
to 30

450 g/1 lb butter
225 g/8 oz caster sugar
2 eggs, separated
grated rind and juice of ½ lemon
675 g/1½ lb plain flour
1 teaspoon baking powder
TOPPING
225 g/8 oz blanched almonds, chopped
a little sugar
ground cinnamon

Beat the butter and sugar together until pale and
creamy. Gradually add the egg yolks, beating continuously until the mixture is creamy. Fold in the
lemon rind and juice, the flour and baking powder.
Mix thoroughly, then cover and chill the dough for
about 2 hours.

Divide the dough into two or three portions, knead
lightly into balls, then roll out on a lightly floured
surface. Use a 5 cm/2 in cutter to cut out the cookies
and place them on greased baking trays. Brush with
the egg whites and sprinkle with chopped almonds,
sugar and a little cinnamon. Bake in a moderate
oven (180C, 350F, gas 4) for 12 to 15 minutes, or
until just beginning to brown. Leave to cool on a
wire rack.

Almond Cookies
**Makes 20
to 30**

3 egg whites
225 g/8 oz caster sugar
350 g/12 oz ground almonds
almond slivers for decoration

Whisk the egg whites until stiff. Gradually add the sugar and ground almonds and mix thoroughly until the mixture is stiff. Using your hands, shape the mixture into a large ball.

Either spoon small amounts of the mixture on to a greased baking tray or shape small portions into balls. Decorate with slivered almonds and bake in a moderate oven (180C, 350F, gas 4) for 10 to 12 minutes, or until golden brown. Leave to cool on a wire rack.

Peanut Cookies
**Makes
about 24**

100 g/4 oz butter
175 g/6 oz sugar
100 g/4 oz smooth peanut butter
1 egg, lightly beaten
2 teaspoons vanilla essence
3 tablespoons milk
275 g/10 oz plain flour
½ teaspoon salt
½ teaspoon baking powder

A good bet with children in the house.

Beat the butter and sugar together until pale and creamy. Add the peanut butter, beating until smooth and creamy. Slowly beat in the egg, vanilla essence and milk, then continue beating until thoroughly combined. Fold in the flour, salt and baking powder, and chill.

Divide the mixture in half. Roll out each piece to give a rectangle measuring 15 × 25 cm/6 × 10 in. Carefully roll up one sheet of the dough (as you would a Swiss roll) and wrap it in cling film. Repeat with the other sheet of dough. Chill for an hour, or until the mixture is firm. When firm, unwrap the rolls and gently reshape them if they have flattened slightly underneath, then cut them into thin slices and place these on greased baking trays.

Bake in a moderately hot oven (190c, 375f, gas 5) for 8 to 10 minutes, or until lightly browned. Leave to cool on a wire rack; the cookies should be swirled like a Swiss roll.

Sarah's Chocolate Chip Cookies

Makes
about 40

225 g/8 oz butter
175 g/6 oz soft brown sugar
175 g/6 oz caster sugar
2 eggs, beaten
1 teaspoon vanilla essence
250 g/9 oz self-raising flour
1 teaspoon baking powder
1 teaspoon bicarbonate of soda
1 teaspoon salt
3(115 g/4 oz) packets chocolate chips

Cream the butter and sugars together until soft. Gradually add the eggs beating continuously, then stir in the vanilla essence. Gently stir in the flour, baking powder, bicarbonate of soda and salt, and mix thoroughly. Stir in the chocolate chips, one packet at a time.

Spoon teaspoonfuls of the mixture on to greased baking trays, keeping them quite small and spaced well apart because the mixture will spread during cooking. Bake in a moderate oven (180c, 350f, gas 4) for 10 to 12 minutes, or until the cookies are golden brown. Allow them to cool slightly on the baking trays before transferring to a wire rack to cool completely.

Hazelnut cookies
Makes
about 24

225 g/8 oz butter	
175 g/6 oz soft brown sugar	
175 g/6 oz caster sugar	
2 eggs, beaten	
1 teaspoon vanilla essence	
250 g/9 oz self-raising flour	
1 teaspoon baking powder	
1 teaspoon bicarbonate of soda	
½ teaspoon ground cinnamon or ground mixed spice	
175 g/6 oz hazelnuts, toasted and chopped	

Beat the butter and sugars together until they are soft and creamy, then gradually beat in the eggs and vanilla. Mix the flour with the baking powder, bicarbonate of soda and salt, then gently stir these dry ingredients into the creamed mixture. Lastly, stir in the nuts.

Place spoonfuls of the mixture well apart on greased baking trays. Bake in a moderate oven (180C, 350F, gas 4) for about 10 to 12 minutes until pale brown. Leave on the trays for a few minutes between transferring them to wire racks to cool completely. Keep making batches until the mixture is used up.

Emma's Chocolate and Walnut Shortbread
Makes 12

175 g/6 oz butter	
75 g/3 oz caster sugar	
250 g/9 oz plain flour	
100 g/4 oz walnuts, chopped	
100 g/4 oz chocolate drops	

Cream the butter and sugar until very pale then mix in the flour, walnuts and chocolate drops. When well combined, lightly press the mixture into a greased oblong tin measuring about 23 × 33 cm/9 × 13 in.

Bake the shortbread in a moderate oven (180C, 350F, gas 4) for 30 minutes until golden. Leave for a few minutes, cut into pieces and leave to cool.

Energy Cookies
Makes 20

175 g/6 oz plain flour
½ teaspoon ground cinnamon
grated rind of 1 orange
25 g/1 oz icing sugar
100 g/4 oz butter
2 carrots, coarsely grated
large handful each of sunflower seeds and raisins

Mix the flour, cinnamon, orange rind and icing sugar. Rub in the butter. Mix in the remaining ingredients.

Roughly divide the mixture into 20 portions, then roll each into a ball and place them slightly apart on greased baking trays. Flatten into circles and bake in a moderately hot oven (200c, 400f, gas 6) for 15 to 20 minutes or until golden brown. Leave on the trays for a minute, then transfer them to a wire rack to cool completely.

Muesli Biscuits
Makes 16

These are the easiest biscuits to make and deliciously chewy to eat. Muesli with plenty of fruit and nuts is best.

225 g/8 oz butter
225 g/8 oz clear honey
100 g/4 oz demerara sugar
225 g/8 oz muesli
225 g/8 oz rolled oats

Melt the butter with the honey and sugar then thoroughly mix in the muesli and oats. Put spoonfuls on to a greased baking tray.

Bake the biscuits in a moderate oven (180c, 350f, gas 4) for 30 minutes until golden. Leave to cool on the tray for a few minutes before transferring to wire racks to cool completely.

Note: If you like the mixture can be pressed into a greased shallow oblong baking tin, then cut into fingers when cold.

Caraway Slices
Makes 20

225 g/8 oz wholemeal flour
pinch of salt
75 g/3 oz sunflower margarine or butter
75 g/3 oz Cheddar cheese, grated
1 teaspoon caraway seeds
1 onion
1 egg yolk

Put the flour and salt in a bowl, then rub in the margarine or butter. Stir in the cheese and caraway seeds. Grate the onion and drain off the juice, add to the mixture. Stir in the egg yolk to make a dough. Alternatively, you can make it in a food processor.

Shape the dough into a roll measuring about 20 cm/8 in long and wrap in cling film. Chill in the refrigerator for 30 to 40 minutes or in the freezer for about 15 minutes, until the dough is really firm. Cut the roll into 20 slices and place these slightly apart on greased baking trays.

Bake in a moderately hot oven (200c, 400f, gas 6) for 15 to 20 minutes or until golden brown. Leave on the tray for a few minutes then transfer the biscuits to a wire rack to cool completely.

Spiced Date Cookies
Makes 16

100 g/4 oz butter
50 g/2 oz caster sugar
175 g/6 oz plain flour
1 teaspoon ground mixed spice
grated rind of 2 oranges
grated rind of 2 lemons
50 g/2 oz dates, chopped
2 tablespoons brandy or rum
50 g/2 oz walnuts, chopped

Cream the butter with the sugar until the mixture is pale and soft. Mix the flour with the spice, then add to the creamed mixture with the orange and lemon rind, dates and brandy. Mix well to form a soft dough.

Roll the mixture out on a floured surface then cut out 16 biscuits and place them slightly apart on greased baking trays. Flatten the biscuits with a fork, then press some walnuts on top of each. Bake in a moderately hot oven (190c, 375F, gas 5) for 15 to 20 minutes or until golden brown. Leave on the tray for a minute, then transfer the biscuits to a wire rack to cool completely.

Florentines

Makes about 18

Marvellous with tea or with coffee instead of a dessert, or with plain vanilla ice cream.

90 g / 3½ oz butter
100 g / 4 oz sugar
150 g / 5 oz mixed nuts (almonds mainly, if possible, mixed with walnuts and hazelnuts)
150 g / 5 oz candied lemon and orange peel, chopped
2 tablespoons double cream

Melt the butter in a saucepan and add the sugar. Stirring all the time, bring slowly to the boil. Remove the pan from the heat and add everything, the cream last. Stir well.

Line baking trays with rice paper, then put tea-spoonfuls of mixture well apart on the paper. Bake in a moderate oven (180c, 350F, gas 4) for about 10 minutes or until lightly brown. Leave to cool slightly on the tins, then remove the florentines to a wire rack to cool completely.

Trim the edges of the cooled rice paper. You can cover the back of the florentines with melted chocolate or just leave them plain. I leave mine plain.

Note: To make an interesting dessert, place florentines all round a serving dish (sticking up). Fill centre with vanilla ice cream.

Port Wine Biscuits

Makes
up to 30

100 g/4 oz butter
100 g/4 oz caster sugar
2 egg yolks
2 tablespoons port
grated rind of 1 orange
225 g/8 oz plain flour
¼ teaspoon cinnamon
salt
¼ teaspoon baking powder
100 g/4 oz ground almonds
100 g/4 oz blanched almonds, chopped
TO FINISH
port for brushing
caster sugar to sprinkle

Cream the butter with the sugar until soft and pale.
Beat in the egg yolks, port and orange rind. Mix in
all the remaining ingredients and take pieces of the
mixture about the size of walnuts. Roll into balls, then
put on greased baking trays and flatten the mixture.
Bake in a moderately hot oven (200c, 400f, gas 6)
for 10 to 12 minutes or until golden. Brush with port
and sprinkle with caster sugar as soon as the biscuits
are removed from the oven, then leave to cool on
wire racks.

Cream Cake

Makes one
20 cm/8 in
cake

250 ml/8 fl oz double cream
2 eggs
225 g/8 oz sugar
200 g/7 oz self-raising flour
½ teaspoon salt
TOPPING
2 tablespoons melted butter
2 tablespoons double cream
50 g/2 oz sugar
50 g/2 oz blanched almonds, slivered
1 tablespoon plain flour

Whip the cream until it holds its shape. Whisk the eggs and sugar together until pale and creamy, then stir them into the cream.

Sift the flour and salt together and fold into the cake mixture. Line a 20 cm/8 in cake tin and grease it thoroughly. Pour the mixture into the tin and bake in a moderate oven (180C, 350 F, gas 4) for 1¼ to 1½ hours or until a skewer inserted into the cake comes out clean. Cover the cake loosely with cooking foil if it starts to brown too quickly during cooking.

For the topping, mix the butter, cream, sugar and almonds in a small saucepan and melt these ingredients over a low heat. Stir in the flour, then spread the topping over the cake and cook for a further 10 minutes. Cool on a wire rack.

My Christmas Cake

Makes a
25 cm/10 in
cake

275 g/10 oz butter
275 g/10 oz sugar
8 eggs
350 g/12 oz self-raising flour
½ teaspoon ground cloves
3 teaspoons mixed spices
1.25 kg/2½ lb mixed dried fruit
225 g/8 oz chopped mixed peel
100 g/4 oz dried apricots
100 g/4 oz almonds, roughly chopped
50 g/2 oz ground almonds
50 g/2 oz walnut pieces
grated rind and juice of 1 orange and 1 lemon
2 tablespoons brandy or rum

You could ice this but I like to leave my cake plain and tie a red ribbon round it.

Beat the butter and sugar together until pale and creamy. Beat in the eggs one at a time adding a teaspoon of flour occasionally to prevent the mixture from curdling. Fold in the rest of the flour and all the remaining ingredients. Mix thoroughly. Line a deep 25 cm/10 in round cake tin with greaseproof paper, and grease it thoroughly. Transfer the mixture to the tin and smooth the top.

Bake in a cool oven (150c, 300f, gas 2) for 4 to 4½ hours, covering the cake with greaseproof paper after the first 2 hours. Allow the cake to cool in the tin for about 30 minutes, then turn it out on to a wire rack to cool completely.

Simple Christmas Cake

Makes a
25 cm/10 in
cake

450 g/1 lb butter or margarine
450 g/1 lb sugar
8 eggs, lightly beaten
450 g/1 lb self-raising flour
225 g/8 oz ground almonds
225 g/8 oz chopped mixed peel
225 g/8 oz glacé cherries, halved
1 kg/2 lb currants

Beat the butter and sugar together in a large mixing bowl until pale and creamy. Gradually add the eggs, beating the mixture continuously and adding a little flour to avoid curdling. Gently fold in the flour and ground almonds (use a metal spoon). Add the mixed peel and cherries to the cake mixture, and, finally, fold in the currants. Gently mix all the ingredients together until the fruit is evenly distributed throughout.

Line a deep round 22–25 cm/9–10 in cake tin and grease it thoroughly. Turn the mixture into the tin, making sure that the mixture is well packed in the tin, then smooth the surface with a small palette knife.

Bake in a cool oven (150c, 300f, gas 2) for 30 minutes, then turn the oven down to very cool (120c, 250f, gas ½) and continue to cook for about a further 3 hours. To test whether the cake is done, insert a skewer in the centre, if it comes out clean the cake is cooked, if not it needs further cooking.

Remove the cake from the oven and leave to cool slightly in the tin before turning it out on to a wire rack to cool completely.

American 1 2 3 4 Cake
Serves 8

Given to me by a friend in America, whose mother gave it to her. Providing you use the same cup throughout, you can't go wrong. Leave it plain or dress it up with anything you fancy.

| 1 cup butter |
| 2 cups sugar |
| 4 eggs |
| 3 teaspoons baking powder |
| 3 cups self-raising flour, sifted |
| 1 teaspoon vanilla extract |
| 1 cup milk |

Cream the butter and sugar thoroughly. Add the eggs, one at a time, beating well. In separate bowls, add the baking powder to the flour and the vanilla to the milk. Add the flour and milk mixtures alternately to the batter, mixing well. Line a 30 cm (12 in) cake tin with greaseproof paper and grease it thoroughly. Pour the mixture into the tin and bake in a moderate oven (180C, 350F, gas 4) for about 50 minutes or until a skewer inserted into the cake comes out clean.

Apple and Cherry Strudel
Serves 6 to 8

| 225 g/8 oz cooking apples |
| 50 g/2 oz caster sugar |
| 300 ml/½ pint water |
| 225 g/8 oz fresh cherries, stoned |
| 50 g/2 oz hazelnuts, chopped and toasted |
| ½ teaspoon ground cinnamon |
| grated rind of 1 orange |
| 8 sheets filo pastry |
| 50 g/2 oz butter, melted |
| GLAZE |
| 2 tablespoons apricot jam |
| 1 tablespoon boiling water |
| icing sugar to sprinkle |
| 50 g/2 oz hazelnuts, chopped and toasted, for topping |

Peel, core and slice the apples, put them in a saucepan. Add the sugar and water. Cook for about 20 minutes or until the fruit is soft and thick. Put the mixture in

a food processor and blend it briefly to make a rough
purée. Stir in the cherries, nuts, cinnamon and orange
rind, then leave to cool completely.

Lay a sheet of pastry, doubled over, on the work
surface. Spread the filling over it up to 2.5 cm/1 in
of the edges. Roll up the pastry to enclose the filling.
Lay another sheet of pastry on the surface and brush
it with a little melted butter, then lift the roll on
to one end and roll it up. Continue rolling the
strudel in the remaining filo, brushing each sheet
with butter.

Put the roll on a greased baking tray and bake in
a moderate oven (180C, 350F, gas 4) for about 20
minutes, or until golden. Transfer to a wire rack.
Sieve the apricot jam and stir in the boiling water,
then brush this over the warm strudel and sift icing
sugar over the top. Sprinkle the nuts on the strudel
and serve warm.

Passion Cake
Makes a
20 cm/8 in
cake

175 g/6 oz butter
175 g/6 oz caster sugar
grated rind of 2 oranges
3 eggs
275 g/10 oz self-raising flour
350 g/12 oz carrots, grated
1 teaspoon ground cinnamon
1 teaspoon grated nutmeg
pinch of ground cloves
225 g/8 oz blanched almonds, chopped
175 g/6 oz sultanas
ICING
225 g/8 oz cream cheese
2 tablespoons frozen concentrated grapefruit juice
1 generous tablespoon icing sugar
freshly grated carrot to decorate

Cream the butter and sugar together until pale and
soft. Beat in the orange rind, then gradually add

the eggs. Fold in the flour, then the carrots with the spices, nuts and fruit. Do not beat the cake mixture at this stage or it will lose all its light airy texture.

Line a 20 cm/8 in deep cake tin with greaseproof paper and grease it thoroughly. Pour the mixture into the tin and bake in a moderate oven (160c, 325F, gas 3) for 1½ hours or until a skewer inserted into the cake comes out clean. Cool the cake on a wire rack.

For the icing beat all the ingredients together and smooth it over the cake. Decorate with grated carrot if you like.

Apple and Pecan Cake
Serves 8

450 g/1 lb self-raising flour
1 teaspoon baking powder
1 teaspoon baking soda
pinch of salt
450 g/1 lb sugar
3 eggs
300 ml/½ pint of sunflower oil
2 teaspoons vanilla extract
450 g/1 lb apples, peeled, cored and chopped
100 g/4 oz chopped pecans
TOPPING
50 g/2 oz brown sugar
50 g/2 oz butter
freshly grated nutmeg
2 tablespoons apple juice

Mix the flour, baking powder, baking soda, salt and sugar. In a separate bowl, beat the eggs and add the oil and vanilla extract. Stir the flour mixture into the eggs and blend well, then add the apples and nuts.

Line an oblong baking tin measuring 30 × 22.5 cm/12 × 9 in with greaseproof paper and grease it. Turn the mixture into the tin and bake in a moderate oven (180c, 350F, gas 4) for 60 minutes, or until a skewer inserted into the cake comes out clean.

To make the topping, heat the sugar, butter, juice and nutmeg in a shallow pan. Boil for about a minute, then pour over the warm cake.

Scripture Cake
Serves 8 to 10

100 g/4 oz butter
175 g/7 oz sugar
50 g/2 oz honey
225 g/8 oz self-raising flour
2 teaspoons baking powder
½ teaspoon ground cinnamon
¼ teaspoon ground cloves
¼ teaspoon ground ginger
¼ teaspoon salt
3 eggs, beaten
100 ml/4 fl oz milk
100 g/4 oz raisins
100 g/4 oz chopped dates
50 g/2 oz chopped figs
100 g/4 oz sliced almonds
1 large apple, peeled and chopped

Cream the butter, sugar and honey together. In a separate bowl, sift the flour, baking powder, spices and salt together. Add half of this to the butter mixture, then add 2 eggs and half the milk. Add the remaining flour mixture, milk and egg and mix well. Stir in the rest of the ingredients, continuing to mix well.

Line a 22.5 × 12.5 cm/ 9 × 5 in rectangular baking tin with greaseproof paper and grease it thoroughly. Pour the mixture into the tin and bake in a moderate oven (160c, 325f, gas 3) for about 2 hours or until a skewer inserted into the cake comes out clean.

This is a recipe that seems to crop up throughout America. Why it is called Scripture Cake I don't know!

Traditional Christmas Dinner

I enjoy Christmas – I've never been one of those people who long to be sitting on a beach on December 25th, as far away from it as possible. I can't wait to do the tree and each year I plan to shop early (and never do!). I also enjoy seeing my family and friends, listening to carols and also cooking a very traditional Christmas meal.

Christmas Turkey

Most people have a favourite way of cooking turkey that they claim is the best. I'm always trying different methods; here are some of my notes. Whichever method you use, make sure the bird is the best and freshest you can buy.

It goes without saying, that it is much better to buy a fresh turkey if you can, rather than a frozen one, as the flavour is much better. However, if you do have a frozen bird, it is most important to make sure that it is completely thawed before cooking. Wipe your turkey inside and out, and sprinkle it with sea salt.

The bird can be stuffed the night before, but the stuffing, if cooked at all, must be completely cold before use. The turkey must not be stuffed any earlier than the night before cooking. The stuffed bird should be smeared with 175 g/6 oz softened butter under the skin covering the breast as well as on top. You may also like to cover the breast with rashers of streaky bacon. Truss the turkey if you want a good shape, wrap the bird loosely in buttered cooking foil and place it in a roasting tin. Keep the turkey chilled until you are ready to cook it.

Roast the turkey for the time given in the chart below, basting it frequently during cooking. About 30 to 40 minutes before the end of the cooking time remove the foil so that the turkey will brown. Allow the cooked turkey to stand in a warm place, wrapped in a clean damp tea-towel, for 15 minutes before carving.

Mix a tablespoon of cornflour or arrowroot with a glass of white wine. Drain any excess grease from the juices left in the roasting tin and place the tin over a medium heat to bring the juices to the boil. Whisk in the wine mixture, and season to taste. Some people always strain the gravy for a smooth result, but I never do.

Roasting Times for Turkey

Weigh the turkey and, following the times given below, roast the bird in a moderate oven (160c, 325f, gas 3).

2.5–3.5 kg/6–8 lb	2¾–3¼ hours
3.5–4 kg/8–10 lb	3¼–3¾ hours
4–6 kg/10–14 lb	3¾–4¼ hours
6–8 kg/14–18 lb	4¼–4¾ hours
8–10 kg/18–20 lb	4¾–5¼ hours

FRUIT STUFFING

1 cooking apple, washed and quartered
1 large orange, wiped and quartered
1 lemon, wiped and quartered
1 onion, peeled
100 g/4 oz chilled butter, diced

Put all the ingredients into the body cavity of the turkey, removing any pips from the fruit. At the end of the roasting time, transfer the turkey to a heated serving dish. Spoon the stuffing out of the bird and place it in a liquidiser or food processor. Process until smooth, then taste for seasoning. Keep the stuffing hot until the turkey is served.

APRICOT, RICE AND NUTS

2 onions, peeled and diced
25 g/1 oz butter
the turkey liver, diced
100 g/4 oz cooked brown rice (slightly undercooked is best)
salt and pepper
75 g/3 oz dried apricots, chopped
75 g/3 oz hazelnuts, halved and toasted
50 g/2 oz raisins
1 egg

Last year I didn't stuff the turkey (I just filled it with chopped up lemons), I made a rice and fruit stuffing separately in a baking tin. I really liked doing it this way - it's worth trying.

Cook the onions in the butter until soft and golden. Add the turkey liver and continue to fry until browned. Stir in the rice, seasoning, apricots, nuts and raisins. Taste and adjust the seasoning if necessary, then stir in the egg. Allow the stuffing to cool, before carefully pressing it into the neck of the turkey (a small metal spoon is best for this).

CHESTNUT STUFFING

1 onion, peeled and chopped
25 g/1 oz butter
225 g/8 oz minced veal or pork sausagemeat
225 g/8 oz unsweetened chestnut purée
75 g/3 oz fresh brown breadcrumbs
1 tablespoon chopped celery
1 egg, beaten
salt and pepper

Cook the onion in the butter until soft. Cool, then mix with the other ingredients and stuff the mixture into the neck of the turkey.

Traditional Sauces

BREAD SAUCE

Serves 8

3 cloves
1 small onion, peeled
1 bay leaf
a few sprigs of parsley
450 ml/¾ pint milk
75 g/3 oz fresh white breadcrumbs
40 g/1½ oz butter
150 ml/¼ pint single cream
salt and pepper
nutmeg to taste

Stick the cloves into the onion and put it in a saucepan with the bay leaf, parsley and milk. Cover and bring slowly to the boil. Remove from the heat and infuse for 30 minutes. Strain, discarding the onion and herbs.

Stir the breadcrumbs and butter into the milk, then cook very gently (use a double saucepan if possible) for 15 minutes. Stir in the cream and add salt, pepper and grated nutmeg to taste. It is important that the sauce is neither too thick nor too bland. Serve with roast turkey, chicken or pheasant.

CRANBERRY SAUCE

Serves 8

225 g/8 oz fresh cranberries
75 g/3 oz caster sugar
150 ml/¼ pint fresh orange juice
large pinch of mixed spice
a little grated orange rind (optional)
1 tablespoon Cointreau or orange liqueur

Put all the ingredients except the orange rind and Cointreau or liqueur into a saucepan and stir well. Cook gently until the cranberries are soft – about 5 minutes. Stir in the orange rind and Cointreau just before serving with roast turkey or game.

The cranberry sauce can be made a couple of days in advance and, when cooled, kept in a covered jar in the refrigerator.

Christmas Goose with Potato Stuffing

Goose is much more fatty than turkey, and does not go nearly as far. Buy a 4.5 kg/10 lb dressed goose for 8 people.

Serves 8

1 young goose (about 4.5 kg/10 lb in weight)
1 tablespoon sea salt
75 g/3 oz butter, softened
2 large onions, finely chopped
450 g/1 lb potatoes
1 large cooking apple, peeled, cored and sliced
6 rindless rashers streaky bacon, diced
3 tablespoons double cream
salt and pepper
150 ml/¼ pint port
600 ml/1 pint good poultry stock
a little arrowroot or cornflour (optional)

Wipe the goose inside and out, and rub both the cavity and skin with the salt. Smear 25 g/1 oz of the butter over the breast.

Cook the onions very slowly in the remaining butter for about 20 minutes, until tender. Meanwhile, boil the potatoes for 10 minutes, then add the apple. Continue cooking for another 5 to 10 minutes, or until both the potatoes and apple are tender. Drain thoroughly and mash together until smooth. Dry-fry the bacon until crisp, then beat it into the potatoes with the cream and onions. Season to taste. Unless you are roasting the goose immediately, allow the stuffing to cool before filling the bird. Stuff the goose from the neck end and sew it up, then stand the bird in a roasting tin. Cover loosely with cooking foil and roast in a moderately hot oven (200C, 400F, gas 6) for 2½ hours, basting frequently.

Remove the foil, tip off the fat and pour the port over the goose. Return to the oven and cook, uncovered, for a further 10 to 15 minutes to crisp the skin. Transfer the goose to a heated serving dish and keep it hot. Pour the stock into the roasting tin and bring the liquid to the boil over a low heat, stirring continuously to remove any meat juices in the tin. If wished, thicken the sauce with a little cornflour or arrowroot blended with 1 or 2 tablespoons of cold water. Strain and pour into a gravy boat.

Christmas Duck
Serves 4

1 fresh duck (about 2.5 kg/5½ lb in weight)
1 teaspoon sea salt
1 orange, pricked all over
3 tablespoons coarse bitter marmalade
2 tablespoons soy sauce
1 small carrot, diced
1 onion, chopped
1 tablespoon flour
2 tablespoons frozen concentrated orange juice
1½ tablespoons lemon juice
300 ml/½ pint poultry stock
1 tablespoon sherry or orange liqueur
pepper

Wipe the duck, inside and out, with a damp cloth. Prick it all over with a fork, then rub the salt all over it, both inside and out. Place the orange inside the duck and leave to stand for 1 hour in a cool place. Stand the duck on a rack in a roasting tin and cook in a moderately hot oven (200c, 400f, gas 6) for 1½ hours, turning the bird every 30 minutes. Start the cooking process with the breast side up, then turn the bird so that it sits on one side, then finally turn it so that it rests on the other side.

Remove the duck from the oven, pour off the fat from the roasting tin leaving the juices in the bottom of the pan. Mix the marmalade and soy sauce and paint half this mixture all over the duck. Put the carrot, onion and liver from the duck into the roasting tin and return it to the oven. Cook for a further 15 to 20 minutes, or until the skin is crisp and browned. Remove the duck, pouring the juices from the body cavity into the tin. Place the bird on a serving dish and keep hot.

Sprinkle the flour into the roasting tin and cook

over a low heat, stirring, until lightly browned. Add the orange juice, lemon juice and stock and bring to the boil, stirring constantly. Simmer for a couple of minutes, then strain this sauce into a small saucepan and add the remaining marmalade mixture, sherry or orange liqueur and pepper to taste. Bring to the boil and tip any juices from the duck into the pan. Serve immediately, with the duck.

Christmas Pudding

Each pudding serves 8

This delicious, fruity yet light pudding, made without flour, is more digestible than traditional rich and heavy puddings.

225 g/8 oz wholemeal breadcrumbs
50 g/2 oz ground almonds
pinch of salt
1 heaped teaspoon ground mixed spice
100 g/4 oz dark soft brown sugar
100 g/4 oz figs, chopped
225 g/8 oz blanched almonds, cut into slivers
100 g/4 oz pine kernels
100 g/4 oz stoned dates, chopped
100 g/4 oz currants
100 g/4 oz sultanas
225 g/8 oz seedless raisins
100 g/4 oz candied peel, chopped
1 large cooking apple, peeled, cored and finely chopped
100 g/4 oz butter, softened
grated rind and juice of 1 lemon
100 g/4 oz set honey
3 eggs, beaten
4 tablespoons brandy

In a large bowl, mix the breadcrumbs, ground almonds, salt, spice, sugar, figs, slivered almonds, pine kernels, dates, the currants, sultanas, raisins, candied peel and the chopped apple.

Cream the butter with the lemon rind and juice and the honey. Gradually beat in the eggs and the brandy.

Stir this mixture into the dry ingredients. When thoroughly mixed, spoon into two 1 kg/2 lb greased pudding basins. Cover with greased greaseproof paper, then cover closely with cooking foil and tie with string. Steam the puddings for 3 hours. Make sure that the water does not evaporate completely during cooking and top up with extra water as necessary.

Allow to cool, then replace the greaseproof paper and foil with fresh covering. Store in a cool dry place. On Christmas day, steam the pudding for a further 3 hours. Turn out the pudding on to a heated serving dish and pour some warmed brandy over it. Immediately set alight and serve while flaming. Serve with Brandy Butter (page 238) or cream.

Try serving Greek yogurt with Christmas pudding instead of the usual cream or brandy butter.

Luxurious Mincemeat
Makes about 8 lb

450 g/1 lb stoned raisins	
450 g/1 lb currants	
450 g/1 lb sultanas	
225 g/8 oz crystallised fruits *or* chopped mixed peel	
175 g/6 oz blanched almonds	
75 g/3 oz walnuts	
175 g/6 oz glacé cherries	
6 cooking apples	
450 g/1 lb dark soft brown sugar	
generous pinch of salt	
grated rind and juice of 2 lemons	
1 teaspoon ground ginger	
1½ teaspoons cinnamon	
1 teaspoon nutmeg	
½ teaspoon ground cloves	
225 g/8 oz butter, melted	
4 large bananas, diced	
300 ml/½ pint brandy	

Wash and thoroughly dry the raisins, currants and sultanas. Finely chop the crystallised fruit (if used). Shred the almonds, and chop the walnuts and cherries. Wash, core and grate the apples with their peel.

Mix all these ingredients in a large mixing bowl with the sugar, salt, lemon rind and juice and the four spices. Pour a quarter of the butter into a non-stick frying pan and, when hot, briefly stir-fry the bananas until they are golden. Add the bananas to the fruit with the remaining butter. Mix well, then stir in the brandy. Store in covered jars for not more than 3 weeks.

Mince Pies
Makes 20 to 24

275 g/10 oz plain flour
25 g/1 oz ground almonds
175 g/6 oz butter, chilled and diced
75 g/3 oz icing sugar, sifted
grated rind of ½ orange
1 egg yolk
3–4 tablespoons orange juice
450 g/1 lb Luxurious Mincemeat (page 236)
a little milk

Put the flour and ground almonds into a mixing bowl. Rub the butter into the flour and almonds until the mixture resembles fine breadcrumbs. Stir in the icing sugar and orange rind.

Mix the yolk with the orange juice and gradually stir it into the mixture to make a soft, but not sticky, dough. Turn out on to a floured surface. Knead gently until smooth, then wrap and chill for 20 to 30 minutes or until firm.

Roll the pastry out to 3 mm/⅛ in thick and cut out 20 to 24 circles large enough to line the base of patty tins. Cut out a further 20 to 24 smaller circles to cover the pies. Line the patty tins with the larger circles of pastry. Put a small spoonful of mincemeat in the pie cases. Brush the edges of the lids with a little cold water and place them on the pies. Press down firmly to seal the edges. Roll out any pastry trimmings and cut out stars or leaf shapes. Cut a small hole in each pie and decorate with the pastry shapes. Brush with a little milk.

If you buy ready-made mince-pies, remove their tops gently and sprinkle the mincemeat with brandy— and replace tops. If they taste good, say you made them!

Bake in a moderate oven (180C, 350F, gas 4) for 15 to 20 minutes until golden brown. Sprinkle with icing sugar and allow to cool in the tins for 5 minutes before transferring to a cooling rack. Store in an airtight tin. Serve hot or cold, with Brandy Butter (below).

Brandy Butter
Serves 6

100 g/4 oz unsalted butter
100 g/4 oz icing sugar, sifted
4 tablespoons brandy

Cream the butter with the sugar until smooth and light, then beat in the brandy. Pile into a small dish to serve.

Christmas Cookies
Makes
about 30

6 eggs
450 g/1 lb dark soft brown sugar
225 g/8 oz plain flour
scant 1 tablespoon ground cinnamon
2 teaspoons ground allspice
225 g/8 oz plain chocolate, grated
225 g/8 oz walnuts, broken
ICING
225 g/8 oz icing sugar
a few drops of lemon juice

Separate two of the eggs and reserve the whites, then beat the yolks with the whole eggs. Gradually mix in the sugar, flour and spices until smooth. Stir in the chocolate and nuts and spread this mixture over a greased and floured 23 × 33 cm/9 × 13 in Swiss roll tin. Bake in a moderate oven (180C, 350F, gas 4) for about 25 to 35 minutes. Cool in the tin, then cut into squares.

To make the icing, sift the icing sugar into a bowl, then gradually beat it into the reserved egg whites until smooth. Stir in the lemon juice. Pipe the icing on the cookies in the shape of initials, names or any decoration of your own choice.

Stollen Bread

250 ml/8 fl oz milk
250 g/9 oz butter
100 g/4 oz caster sugar
25 g/1 oz dried yeast
6 tablespoons tepid water
675 g/1½ lbs strong white flour
pinch each of salt, mace and nutmeg
2 eggs, lightly beaten
175 g/6 oz chopped mixed peel
100 g/4 oz sultanas
25 g/1 oz walnuts, chopped
25 g/1 oz blanched almonds, chopped
75 g/3 oz stoned dates or apricots, chopped
4 tablespoons runny honey
4 tablespoons light soft brown sugar
pinch of cinnamon

Bring the milk to the boil, then add the butter and sugar and stir, off the heat, until melted. Allow to cool until just warm. Sprinkle the yeast over the water, adding a pinch of sugar, and stir well. Leave until frothy, then add to the milk mixture. Sift half the flour, the salt and the spices into a bowl. Make a well in the middle and add the eggs with the yeast mixture. Beat very thoroughly, either by hand or in a food mixer using a dough hook. Gradually add the remaining flour to make a soft dough, then knead it thoroughly using a dough hook or by hand (it will take about 7 to 8 minutes). The dough should be smooth and not at all sticky.

Have you ever made a bread and butter pudding with Stollen bread? Try it — it's great!

Place the dough in an oiled bowl, cover and leave in a warm place until doubled in volume. Turn the dough out on to a floured surface, add the peel, sultanas, chopped nuts and the dates or apricots. Knead well, working in the fruit, until all the ingredients are fully incorporated. Divide the dough in half and shape each portion into an oval. Place the two loaves on greased baking trays, cover with oiled polythene and leave in a warm place for about 1½ hours or until doubled in size.

Bake the loaves in a moderately hot oven (200C, 400F, gas 6) for 15 minutes, then reduce the oven temperature to moderate (180C, 350F, gas 4) and bake for a further 25 minutes. Five minutes before the end of the cooking time drizzle the honey over the loaves and sprinkle with the sugar mixed with the cinnamon. Replace the loaves in the oven to finish cooking, then cool them on a wire rack.

Serve within 24 hours, or freeze the loaves for up to 3 months.

Note: If you like add a few glacé cherries to the mixture and drizzle white glacé icing over the cooled loaves. Decorate with halved glacé cherries and strips of angelica.

Boxing Day Carrot Cake
Makes one
20 cm/8 in
cake

2 tablespoons orange juice
1 tea bag
150 g/5 oz icing sugar
4 eggs
350 ml/12 fl oz sunflower oil
300 g/11 oz plain flour
1½ teaspoons baking powder
1 teaspoon each ground cinnamon and allspice
2 teaspoons grated orange rind
225 g/8 oz carrots, grated
100 g/4 oz walnuts, chopped
icing sugar to dust the cake

Heat the orange juice, then pour it over the tea bag and leave to cool while making the cake mixture. Whisk the sugar and eggs together until pale and thick, gradually adding the oil. In a separate bowl, mix the flour, baking powder, spices and orange rind, then fold this mixture, a tablespoon at a time, into the eggs.

Fold the carrots into the cake with the orange juice and walnuts. Pour into a well-greased 20 cm/8 in cake tin and bake in a moderate oven (180c, 350f, gas 4) for 1½ hours, or until the cake is firm to the touch and a skewer inserted into the middle comes out clean.

Leave to cool on a wire rack, then sprinkle with icing sugar.

Mulled Wine
Serves 12

1 orange
1 lemon
2 bottles red wine
2 long cinnamon sticks (about 7.5 cm/3 in)
4 cloves
100 g/4 oz sugar
6 tablespoons water
pinch of mixed spice

Pare all the rind from both the orange and the lemon, taking care not to include any of the pith. Place the fruit rinds in a saucepan with the wine and all the remaining ingredients, then simmer gently for 5 minutes.

Café Brûlot
Serves 6

2 teaspoons sugar
1 small cinnamon stick
grated rind of 1 small orange
¼ teaspoon ground cloves
6 tablespoons cognac, warmed
900 ml/1½ pints freshly made strong coffee
a little lightly whipped cream (optional)

Mix all the ingredients (except the cream) in a warmed bowl and serve in heatproof glasses. Top each serving with a little cream if you like.

Christmas Grog
Serves 6

750 ml/1¼ pints boiling water
2 orange pekoe tea bags
150 ml/¼ pint rum
2 tablespoons brown sugar
pinch of cinnamon

Pour the boiling water over the tea bags and set aside to cool. Strain the tea into a saucepan and add all the remaining ingredients. Heat through and serve in mugs.

Christmas Cheating

- Buy the very best Christmas pudding available
  and prick it all over with a skewer, then pour
  plenty of brandy or rum into it and wrap it
  tightly in cooking foil. If you have time repeat
  this process over a few days.

- The best quality bought Christmas cake can
  be treated in the same way as the Christmas
  pudding. Turn the cake upside-down and pierce
  it all over with a skewer, then trickle plenty
  of brandy over the surface. Wrap the cake in
  cooking foil and repeat if you have time.

- Shop bought mincemeat can be enlivened by
  adding brandy or rum and some grated orange
  or lemon rind. If you are really stuck for time,
  buy the best mince pies you can find. Carefully
  lift off their lids and spoon a little brandy over
  the filling. Serve home-made brandy or rum
  butter with the warmed pies.

- If you don't have the time to prepare your
  own mayonnaise, then buy the best available
  and add a little double cream just as you are
  using it.

- Simple casseroles can be varied and made more
  elaborate by adding interesting ingredients:
  try dried apricots, halved walnuts or shredded
  orange or lemon rind. You can freeze a simple
  meat or poultry casserole well in advance, then
  by adding something extra about 15 minutes
  before serving you can transform it into a nice
  meal just when you're in a panic.

Happy Endings

*I have never liked large New Year's Eve
celebrations with lots of noise and shouting,
when you suddenly find yourself linking arms
with a total stranger to sing Auld Lang Syne.
I like to see the old year out with best friends
and loved ones around me – so I have arranged
a New Year's Eve menu that will work
equally well for my type of party or for a large
celebration if you prefer.*

*Here are some ideas that you can adapt or
which, at the very least, will set you thinking.*

Menu

Coulibiac
*
Cabbage Filled with Dip
*
Big Green Salad
*
Tremendous Trifle

Coulibiac

Serves 8

This Russian fish pie is traditionally served at weddings and celebration feasts.

50 g/2 oz butter
2 large onions, finely chopped
350 g/12 oz mushrooms, sliced
175 g/6 oz long-grain rice
2 tablespoons chopped parsley or tarragon
450 g/1 lb cooked fresh salmon
2 tablespoons lemon juice
3 hard-boiled eggs, sliced
salt and pepper
450 g/1 lb puff pastry (you can use a 454 g/1 lb packet frozen pastry, thawed, or your own home-made)
beaten egg to glaze

Melt the butter in a frying pan, add the onions and cook slowly until soft. Add the mushrooms and stir-fry over low heat for 2 minutes. Remove from the heat and allow to cool. Meanwhile, cook the rice in boiling salted water until tender. Rinse and drain thoroughly, then add to the onion mixture with the parsley or tarragon.

Remove the skin and bones from the salmon and flake the fish. Add the lemon juice, then add the fish to the onion and rice mixture. Slice the hard-boiled eggs and add to the filling with the seasoning. Gently mix all the ingredients together.

Roll out the pastry 5 mm/¼ in thick to give a rectangle
measuring about 42.5 × 25 cm/17 × 10 in. Trim the edges. (Reserve the trimmings and use them for the decoration.) Brush the pastry with a little beaten egg. Spoon the salmon mixture on to the pastry, moulding it into a neat mound with your hands. Fold the long edges of the pastry up over the filling, to meet and overlap in the middle. Brush the pastry with egg between the overlap and fold the ends in to seal the coulibiac. Transfer to a greased baking tray, making sure the seam is underneath. Brush all over with egg.

Use the pastry trimmings to decorate the coulibiac and make a small hole in the middle of the pastry to allow the steam to escape. Bake in a moderately hot oven (200c, 400f, gas 6) for about 30 minutes, or until golden brown and well puffed.

To serve, cut into thick slices and serve very hot with a bowl of chilled soured cream handed separately. Alternatively the coulibiac can be served cold with the cucumber and soured cream dip.

Cabbage Filled with Dip
Serves 8

300 ml / ½ pint soured cream
1 tablespoon finely chopped radish
1 tablespoon finely chopped chives
150 ml / ¼ pint mayonnaise
1 small cucumber, grated
100 g / 4 oz salted cashew nuts, chopped

Mix the soured cream with the radish and chives, then stir in the mayonnaise. Squeeze out all the liquid from the cucumber – do this with your hands – then add the grated cucumber to the dip. Stir in the nuts and chill lightly.

Cut out the middle of a large cabbage and find a basin or bowl which will fit into the cavity. Leave the outer leaves of the cabbage to surround the bowl.

Spoon the dip into the bowl and place it in the middle of the cabbage to serve. Complete the decoration, if you like, by inserting fresh flowers or cheese crackers in between the leaves of the cabbage.

Big Green Salad

A large, healthy green salad always goes down well at a party, but make sure that all the ingredients are shredded or chopped finely enough to be eaten without difficulty using just a fork.

Use as many different types of lettuce as you like – the more varied the better – or Chinese cabbage or endive. Add shredded spring onions, finely sliced green peppers, alfalfa or bean sprouts, strips of cucumber and sliced avocado pears. Any other green vegetables can be added.

Toss all the ingredients together in a large bowl, remembering to add the avocados at the last minute so that they won't have time to discolour. Serve your favourite dressing to accompany the salad or make a simple vinaigrette.

Bryan's Tremendous Trifle
Serves 30

FIRST LAYER
16 trifle sponges (2 packets)
300 ml / ½ pint sherry, Cointreau, Kirsch or other liqueur
SECOND LAYER
1 kg / 2 lb exotic fruit, peeled and stoned (for example, kiwis, lychees and mangoes)
THIRD LAYER
900 ml / 1½ pints milk
large vanilla pod
90 g / 3½ oz caster sugar
6 teaspoons cornflour
6 eggs
FOURTH LAYER
pared rind and juice of 3 lemons
350 ml / 12fl oz sherry or white wine
6 tablespoons brandy
225 g / 8 oz caster sugar
900 ml / 1½ pints double cream
DECORATION
sugared almonds
kiwis slices
angelica strips

Line a very large dish with the trifle sponges and soak them in the sherry or liqueur. Cover these with the prepared fruit.

For the next layer, heat the milk with the vanilla pod in a large heavy-based saucepan. Mix the sugar with the cornflour and eggs. Pour on a little of the hot milk, stir well and pour the mixture into the saucepan with the rest of the milk. Stir constantly over a moderate heat until it thickens; do not boil. Strain, pour over the fruit and cool.

For the next layer, place the lemon rind and juice in a bowl with the sherry or wine and the brandy. Cover tightly and leave to stand while the custard is cooling. Strain this mixture, discard the lemon rind and mix the liquid with the sugar, stirring until it dissolves. Gradually stir in the cream, then whisk the mixture until it stands in soft peaks. Spoon this syllabub over the trifle. Decorate and chill.

Index